SHROPS

MURDER
CASEBOOK

PAUL HARRISON

COUNTRYSIDE BOOKS
NEWBURY · BERKSHIRE

SHROPSHIRE
MURDER CASEBOOK

COUNTRYSIDE BOOKS
3 Catherine Road
Newbury, Berkshire

ISBN 1 85306 321 5

Produced through MRM Associated Ltd., Reading
Typeset by Paragon Typesetters, Queensferry
Printed by Woolnough Bookbinding, Irthlingborough

Dedication

To Barbara Billing, Ian Oliver, Neil Cowley, Mark Britt, Pete Wragg, Eddie Silber, Kevin Burton, Ray Wilson, Geoff Gent, Mick Jeffery, Ian Hopkins, Katie Gingell, Bob Britchford, Michael Norris. Otherwise known as 'the staff of Rota 4', Kettering. Simply the best!

Contents

Introduction and Acknowledgements   8

1. With Malice Aforethought   11

2. The Murder Team   35

3. A Butcher's Revenge   42

4. Only The Strong Survive   49

5. Death of a Marriage   55

6. The Church Stretton Axe Murders   58

7. The Caroline Carver Mystery   64

8. Deadly Love   71

9. Traumatic Toothache!   77

10. The Pin-stripe Jacket Mystery   81

11. Drunk and Disorderly   88

12. Murder at Rhos Cottage   95

13. The Black Panther   100

14. The Hilda Murrell Case   110

15. The Heath House Murder Mystery   116

Introduction and Acknowledgements

A book upon death and destruction should not be categorised as light reading, and I hope that those who read this latest volume in the Countryside Murder Casebook series will enjoy it but not dwell too deeply upon the human depravity it contains.

Murder is perhaps over-dramatised in today's society, we read about it and see it upon the screens of our televisions in either fact or fictional format. Yet murder is a fairly infrequent occurrence, and is generally as a result of domestic situations. There are not too many British murderers who escape justice, especially so with today's modern policing methods.

In Shropshire you are fortunate to be policed by some of the finest male and female officers in the country, the West Mercia force is held in high regard throughout the British Isles. But what should be remembered is that they depend upon you every bit as much as you depend upon them, so if you see something suspicious, report it to the police; your assistance makes it all the easier to catch criminals.

The criminals discussed in this work are unique, all have been tried for murder of a fellow human being, or in some cases, more than one. Their crimes should help us learn and understand the complexities of the human mind, just what makes a perfectly normal individual kill another. Unfortunately, there are no hard and fast rules when it comes to murder, literally, anything goes, and very rarely does a premeditated crime go as planned, which makes it all the more intriguing.

I have thoroughly enjoyed researching and writing this work, the people of Shropshire have been unbelievably helpful, and without you I could never have completed it. I would also like to pass my wholehearted appreciation to the news-room staff of the *Shrewsbury Chronicle* who kindly allowed me to conduct research from their newspaper archives. I would also like to acknowledge the staffs of the *Shropshire Star* and the Shropshire Express and Star newspapers for their kind assistance with illustrations and extend my thanks to Jillian Harrison for her help. To the West Mercia police for their kind assistance and suggestions during the research for this work. To Nicholas and Suzanne Battle for their continuing support and belief in the Murder Casebook project, to David Graves for putting it all together, and to my wife Lesley, for her kind understanding and support, and to anyone else I may have omitted.

Paul Harrison
Kettering 1994

1

WITH MALICE AFORETHOUGHT

For most people murder has a morbid fascination. Perhaps it is the often horrendous circumstances in which one human being terminates the life of another. Some believe that people enjoy reading a 'good' murder to satisfy their blood lust, in some cases this may be so, but most people are intrigued by the actions of the killer rather than the basic blood and guts of the affair.

It is only natural that those who possess enquiring minds should question the reasons for acts which are to most of us, unnatural. Despite the high media coverage of murders, the unlawful killing of one human being by another does not occur in today's society with alarming frequency. Certainly, when one compares statistics with previous centuries then the 20th century has far less, even allowing for the fact that such figures for crime cannot be accurately assessed as many murders in previous centuries went unrecorded. Those were the times when good was good and bad was evil; if one transgressed the trust or the basic laws of the land then you were punished, often extremely harshly, execution was more than a possibility!

Executions were at one time a public affair, carried out in well-known locations so that as many people as possible could attend and witness the termination of human life, but not just a human life; such executions were deemed to be the elimination of an evil source placed upon the earth to commit atrocities against their fellows. Men, women and children attended the executions, which were seen as a source of family enjoyment. By the early part of the 19th century, broadsheets were being produced and sold at executions.

These, also known as 'penny dreadfuls', generally consisted of a single sheet of paper upon which was printed the basic dramatised account of the awful deed committed by the individual awaiting execution. Occasionally the retelling of the events was loosely

11

formed to read like a poem or a song! At the top of the sheet would be a crude illustration, of either the crime in commission stage, or an execution scene. Very often, these illustrations or woodcuts as they were commonly known, would be utilised for a number of crimes or executions. The broadsheets were produced by a number of different printers, the most infamous of whom was Jeremy Catnach, a northerner who moved to London and commenced trading in Monmouth Court, Seven Dials in 1813. Catnach was a prolific printer of broadsheets which provided a reasonable profit, indeed, it has been claimed that Catnach made in excess of £500 profit from the sales of one individual broadsheet. Catnach was also known as 'Old Jemmy' and when he died in 1841 the business continued, being run by his sister Anne Ryle along with another partner, James Paul. This business lasted just four years until 1845 when the partnership was abandoned.

Executions in the county of Shropshire occurred in a variety of locations in the 17th and 18th centuries. As late as the 19th century in some cases the perpetrator would be executed close to where the crime occurred; portable gallows were used for this purpose. Containing the spectators at executions was a major operation, very often the excited or agitated crowd would surge forward in an attempt to get as close to the gallows as possible. All too often innocent people were crushed or trampled to death. The main locale of execution in Shropshire was Shrewsbury, but most of the larger towns had their fair share of such executions. These were the days when law and order were in their infancy, in fact, one could virtually say that law and order in the form we now recognise did not exist.

One of the earliest cases of barbarous murder recorded within the county of Shropshire occurred in the 17th century, the information regarding dates and precise locations is extremely vague, but it does produce a marvellous image of how life was in those long ago times, and just how rotten society could be.

Jocelin Harwood was born of a reasonably well-to-do family at Wateringbury, Kent in 1669, his parents making every possible effort to ensure that Jocelin was given the opportunities to start a good and decent life.

In 1686, Harwood turned his back upon his parents, when at the age of just 17 he ran away from home taking with him the princely sum of £60, which in those times was a small fortune. It is not clear whether he stole this from his parents, but it does seem more than likely. Fleeing to London, Harwood quickly fell in with the wrong crowd who avidly assisted him in spending his money, which was wasted on alcohol, women and luxuries for his new found associates. With the money spent, he found himself a lonely young man: he had enjoyed being the centre of attention and resolved to regain his former financial status. This was not achieved in any lawful manner, but by theft which would more often than not include violence.

By 1690, having found the picking of pockets and petty pilfering financially unrewarding, he took to greater and more daring crimes. Stealing a horse and all the accoutrements necessary for riding such an animal, he further stole a couple of pistols and set out for Black Heath. Once there he attempted to hold up two gentlemen en route for the city of London. He cried out 'Stand and deliver', but neither gentleman did as was asked of them; indignantly they produced pistols which they fired at Harwood. In the ensuing melee Harwood's mount was shot and fell wounded. In sheer terror, Harwood fired back, causing slight injuries to the two men. He then fled the scene, without a horse and without any valuables; even worse, with his pride in tatters.

Over the months which followed, Harwood became a little more astute in the ways of highway robbery as he moved all over the south of England, committing thousands of crimes over a period of about four years. So renowned was his reputation in the south of England that other highwaymen and women elected to finish him off themselves.

But Harwood was a determined villain; by 1692 he was concentrating his efforts upon the county of Shropshire. Word had reached him that a certain house in the county contained many treasures which were largely left unguarded. The house belonged to Sir Nehemiah Burroughs, its precise location is not recorded. One evening, along with two other reprobates, Harwood broke into the premises and made immediately for the servants' quarters. Once there the innocent staff were attacked, bound and gagged to prevent them raising any alarm.

With this achieved Harwood searched the house until he located Burroughs and his wife, whom he also secured with rope. Next he moved into the room occupied by the two daughters of Burroughs. It was then that Harwood's mind apparently snapped. One of the girls said to him, 'Pray, sir, use us civilly, for if you do, we will use you in the same manner, in case you and your companions are taken, for I am sure we shall know you again!' 'Shall you so?' replied Harwood, 'I'll take care then, to prevent you doing any mischief.' With this, he drew his sword and slit both the girls' throats before violently slashing at their unprotected bodies. Incensed, he then ran through to the room where Sir Nehemiah and his wife were incapacitated and screamed at them both, 'What, and do you know me too?' The couple attempted to placate him, telling him that they did not. 'Damn you, you are only a little more artful than your daughters, but I shan't trust you.'

With this he produced his blood-stained sword and ran it straight through the couple again and again until they were so severely wounded that it would have been impossible for them to survive. Collecting the valuables from the house he then fled.

Unbeknown to Harwood, his two colleagues were so mortified and provoked by his actions that they decided to hand him over to justice themselves. As they rode away from the scene of carnage at the Burroughs' household, one of them shot dead Harwood's horse; they then leapt upon Harwood and bound him hand and foot and left him by the side of the road. In order to connect him with the murder at the Burroughs' residence, they left some of the stolen property next to him.

The following day both Harwood and the murders were discovered; he was at once taken to Shrewsbury gaol escorted by several guards, en route there he was abusive towards his captors and mankind in general. He was subsequently tried at Shrewsbury and continued to hurl abuse and profanities at the judge and jury. It was even claimed that he spat at them! He was found guilty of murder and sentenced to hang by the neck until dead, afterwards his body was to be hung in chains on a gibbet as the ultimate humiliation, and to serve as a warning to other would-be criminals. Before execution, Harwood declared that he would commit the same crime again if he were ever given the opportunity; moments later he was swinging from the hangman's rope, dead.

Such an incident must evoke emotions of horror and disbelief in the reader, but it should not go unnoticed that Harwood's companions acted in a commendable manner, albeit they had committed a serious crime, but they realised the value of life and just how dangerous Harwood was. In their own way they acted in a responsible manner, almost as agents of law and order.

Harwood was not the only villain loose within the boundaries of Shropshire around this same era, for Harvey Hutchins was creating something of a poor reputation for himself. Hutchins was born in 1678 to good stock, his father being a sword-blade maker, his mother skilled in the manufacture of clothing. Like so many youngsters hailing from good solid family backgrounds, Hutchins was apprenticed out to a silversmith in Shrewsbury, but chose to steal a great deal from his master and so ended up in gaol.

As if this punishment was insufficient to teach the young Hutchins a lesson, once released he committed further thefts in the county, before fleeing to London as a place of sanctuary more than anything else.

In London, Hutchins prepared himself for the nerve-racking life associated with hardened criminals. He made up his mind that he was going to be one of the most revered villains in England, and so took in with a dastardly crowd who stole for a master thief known as Constantine.

Constantine took a liking to the young Hutchins and taught him all he knew about crime, stealing, handling and selling stolen goods, until within a few years Hutchins had earned himself the respect of many of London's criminal fraternity. With such a reputation behind him, Hutchins worked alone and carried out many daring thefts; admittedly he was often caught and served his time in Newgate prison and other such salubrious London locations. Eventually, he was apprehended after having committed a much publicised burglary of a Jew's home in Duke's Place. For this he was sentenced to death and executed at Tyburn in 1704. It has been said that at his execution several members of the criminal fraternity who knew Hutchins, openly wept at the sad loss of an expert criminal! So much of an expert was he that he was caught and prevented from committing further crimes against an innocent public. His captors were in all probability petty criminals themselves, as the dividing line between crime and law and order in the 18th century was virtually non-existent, and bribery of officers of the crown was a reasonably common event. Similarly anyone who posed a threat, be it personal or general would be sought out; society was beginning to realise that there were too many bad people in the world, and someone had to determine just who these people were and to prevent them from committing crimes and ruining lives.

In the beginning

The origins of policing in England and Wales can be traced back to the Danish and Anglo-Saxon eras. The Saxons introduced into their hectic society a tythingman or borsholder or even headborough. Ranking above him was the office of hundred man and shire reeve (sheriff). These persons were empowered to collect taxes and to enforce law and order as best they could. By 1252 the term 'constable' was introduced and is believed to come from the term

'Comes Stabuli', Master of Horse, an embodiment of both royal and communal authority. The officer was elected annually by the local community and was seen as having something of a good social status.

In 1258 came the introduction of the 'Statute of Winchester' which provided further powers to the constable. Watchmen were employed to assist the constable during the execution of his duties, and a watch, consisting of up to 16 men would be deployed at each gate to the respective towns. These persons were given power to arrest felons, strangers or anyone they deemed to be transgressing the rules of their masters. In the majority of towns, almost every male resident was more or less conscripted to this duty at some time.

For some reason, perhaps because there were too many other bodies acting as agents of the law, the position of constable deteriorated in status, until it was of no importance whatsoever: the constable was an isolated figure who could be dodged with some ease, but the watchmen were a force that could apprehend villains purely by superior numbers and their dominating presence.

Later the powers afforded to a constable, which had always been at Common Law, were gradually extended with the assistance of an Act of Parliament which stated:

'You shall swear that you shall keep the peace of our Lord the King well and lawfully according to your power, and shall arrest all those who shall make any contest, riot, debate, or affray, in breaking the said peace and shall bring them into the house or compter of one of the sheriffs. And if you shall be withstood by strength of such misdoers, you shall raise upon them hue and cry shall follow them from street to street from ward to ward until they are arrested. And also you shall search at all times when you shall be required by scavager [toll collector] or Bedel [beadle], for the common nuisances of the ward, until they be arrested.'

Incredibly, the constable's role remained virtually unchanged for almost 500 years!

The basis of this Act directed that prisoners should be detained at the constable's house until such time as the case had been heard, the felon tried and judgement passed. Any expense incurred during this detention was the sole responsibility of the constable! It is therefore easy to see why this post was such an unpopular one. In reality the constables were low in the social structure. Sheriffs were deemed to be of a higher rank, so would instruct the constable to keep the prisoner at his home, whereas a constable had no one beneath him to whom he could pass the responsibility!

The term 'hue and cry' was a system devised to assist agents of the law in the apprehension of escaping felons, the system worked in a very basic way and relied upon everyone else in the area being law-abiding citizens. Theoretically, the prisoner or felon flees from the scene of a crime, pursued by the constable or watchmen. As they gave chase through the streets they were to make such a commotion, shouting out to stop the offender, until a crowd was also giving chase and the individual hunted down. The chase would continue until the felon was captured through either tiredness or a mistaken move. Very probably in the 20th century such principles would be greatly appreciated by the police, although the public in general are of great assistance in the fight against crime.

Public assistance was never more obvious than in an awful case which occurred in the village of Dorrington, to the south of Shrewsbury in 1787. Had it not been for the vigilance and honesty of certain individuals a despicable crime would have gone unsolved. Once again, full details are sketchy, as the concept of keeping detailed records of such crimes was virtually unrecognised.

One morning, residents of Dorrington village, noticing that the shop of Mary Davies had not been opened made further investigations. The rear door to her house was ajar; it gave access to the coal house and then the kitchen area. As the door swung open the awful sight which revealed itself to those who were at the scene was virtually unforgettable. There upon the stone floor lay the body of Mary Davies; her head was split wide open and brain tissue spilled out of the gaping wound. Close by was a coal axe, the obvious murder weapon. The killer had not been satisfied with leaving the body as it lay, but had placed a large lump of coal on her head, further diminishing the dead woman's dignity.

The search was on for a ruthless, brutal killer. A rushed inquest brought in a verdict of wilful murder by person(s) unknown. Before long a suspect had been identified; a traveller from Shrewsbury informed the authorities that he had met Sarah Turner, alias Marygold, who had told him of her wicked plan, but he had not anticipated that she would carry it out. Apparently, Turner had little or no money to pay for her lodgings, but had returned to Shrewsbury the following day with an abundance of coins, sufficient to pay for more than one night's accommodation.

Turner was arrested and committed to Shrewsbury gaol; at her trial she was found guilty of murder and subsequently confessed to the crime. She claimed that having been unable to pay for her lodgings in Shrewsbury, she visited Dorrington and the home of Mrs Davies, which was also a lodging house, and acquired a room for the night. At eight o'clock the following morning Davies had ordered Turner to get up. Turner had been sleeping in a room partitioned by a sheet strung from a cord across the room. Having got up and in a bad mood, she cut the cord supporting the sheet which fell to the ground. Mary Davies was sat huddled over the kitchen fire, her back to Sarah Turner. The lodger then cut the cord once again until it was small enough to manage. She then placed it around Mary Davies' neck and throttled her until she thought she was dead. Turner was shocked when her victim revived and begged for mercy; it was too late. Sarah Turner was frightened of being reported and so dragged Davies to the coalhouse where she put the coal axe through her skull. She then stole almost £10 from the house and fled, back to Shrewsbury where she was arrested the following week, and her dastardly deed received its justly deserved punishment.

The same cannot be said of a crime which took place in Oswestry the following year, 1788, when father and son, both of whom were called Thomas Phipps, were executed at Shrewsbury. Thomas Phipps senior was aged 48 years and junior aged just 20; they hailed from Llwney Mapsis near Oswestry. The crime was of no significance, albeit deceitful and cunning, but no physical injury was caused to anyone, yet the men were executed in such a dramatic manner that it cannot be ignored in a work such as this. The brief details of the crime indicate that the men were found guilty of printing and issuing a £20 note knowing it to be forged. Both men were tried at Shrewsbury and found guilty of the crime and sentenced to execution. Later, too late for reprieve, the younger Thomas Phipps admitted that his father was unaware of the forgery and was thus innocent of the crime.

On the day of execution they were taken by mourning coach accompanied by a clergyman and a friend, to where the gallows stood waiting for them. As they approached Thomas Phipps senior said to his son, 'Tommy thou hast brought me to this shameful end, but I forgive thee. Thou hast brought me hither, dost thou lead the way?' The son climbed down from the coach and ascended the ladder on to the scaffold followed by his allegedly innocent father. It was a joint execution in which both men were to swing together; they stood above the trap door, and in the final few seconds before the bolt was drawn, father and son embraced each other and together dropped into eternity, still clutching one another. It was a dramatic scene and one which evoked great pity from the spectators, many of whom openly cried. Seldom in the history of the gallows can there have been a more emotionally moving execution.

Law and order was perilously capricious during those times, and continued to be so until the Municipal Corporation Act of 1835 brought some improvement, though even then it was debatable as to whether this was an actual step forward. The Act was not primarily brought about to introduce policing strategies, but was a set of rules for councils to act upon, one of which was the maintenance of a police force. It took until February 1836 for anything tangible to occur in Shrewsbury, when the watch committee informed the council that they had appointed 13 constables for duty, four as daytime police officers and nine as night-watchmen. Within twelve months, one of the four policemen had resigned taking a better post elsewhere. The force complement was maintained at three daytime officers, the fourth man's wages being split between the remaining trio. The following year, 1838, one of the trio died, leaving just two officers to shoulder the responsibilities of the Shrewsbury Borough Force.

Elsewhere, at Bridgnorth matters were dealt with more seriously; ten officers were sworn in as constables by mid-January 1836. The boroughs of Oswestry, Wenlock and Ludlow also took on several constables within their perimeters. It should be stressed that although officially provided with the title of constable, these officers were a far cry from being an organised body of men, albeit the ranks of superintendent and sergeant were introduced. Their duties still included collecting taxes and acting as general dogsbody for the councils as well as attempting to maintain law and order. Slight improvement had been made by the provision of lock-ups to house prisoners!

The provision of local borough forces was all very well, but the more rural areas of Shropshire, where footpads, or even highwaymen could loiter, left much to be desired; these areas had no cover or policing whatsoever. Hence the formation of the Shropshire Constabulary, to police rural districts.

The first Chief Constable of the Shropshire Force was Captain Dawson Mayne, RN, who was the younger brother of the Metropolitan Police Commissioner, Sir Richard Mayne. Mayne had served in the Royal Navy between 1812 and 1834. During the period 1840 to 1843 the county and borough forces were pushed to their limits; Shropshire, a county not normally noted for brutality or acts of barbarity, had three notable serious offences which severely tested the astuteness of the respective police forces.

In autumn 1840 a most horrific assault took place in the pleasant surroundings of Ludlow at the Angel Hotel. The offender in this brutal crime was a nondescript from Birmingham. Joseph Mister was a 25 year old petty criminal, virtually a vagrant, but not the sort of vagrant who would wander the countryside but rather the streets of Birmingham and the Midlands area.

Mister heard of the presence of a certain John Ludlow, a travelling man who had earned his fortune from selling cattle. Rumour had it that Ludlow carried with him a small fortune in ready cash, a natural enticement for a would-be thief. Mister made his way to Shropshire and located Ludlow at the Unicorn in Shrewsbury, where he usually always slept in the same room. Fortunately for Ludlow, he moved rooms on this occasion and the planned robbery failed as Mister was unable to locate the room his quarry slept in.

The pursuit continued to the town of Ludlow and the Angel Hotel. Mister knew that John Ludlow, a creature of habit, again slept in a specific room at the hotel, and thus secreted himself in there before any of those attending the hotel's social gathering retired to their rooms. For reasons unknown, be it fate or otherwise, Ludlow did not sleep in his usual room; instead a commercial traveller named William Mackereth took it. The scene was set.

Around four o'clock in the morning William Mackereth awoke with a start; he had felt someone or something touching his neck. Instinctively he put his hands to his neck but half asleep felt nothing untoward. Moments later he felt it again; in panic and sheer terror he jumped out of bed and ran to the window of the room which fronted on to the main street. The window was shut tight and Mackereth could not budge it; clutching on to the curtains he smashed the window with his free hand and shouted for help before rushing to the door and out into the main corridor of the hotel, all the time shouting for assistance. Mr Cooke, the landlord of the hotel, rushed to Mackereth's aid, and was astounded to see his guest standing there with blood spurting out of several wounds to his face and neck.

Amazingly, perhaps through shock, Mackereth seemed oblivious to this. He was taken back to his room and placed back in bed, and as death seemed imminent a deposition was recorded in front of several witnesses. More curious were the circumstances surrounding the incident. Mr Cooke had initially believed that Mackereth had tried to take his own life, but this was not the story being told by the wounded man.

Blood covered the walls and floor of Mackereth's room, and a black-handled cut-throat razor was found in the yard outside the hotel; this was seized by Constable Hammond as the probable weapon used during the incident. The majority of guests in the hotel were awakened by the commotion and offered to carry out a search of the premises and surrounding area for the attacker or possible evidence; that is, all but one guest – Joseph Mister remained in his room!

The police constables who visited the scene of the attack observed that dust beneath the bed had been disturbed suggesting that someone had recently lain there. The realisation dawned upon those present that someone had attempted to murder Mackereth, but for what reason?

The police instructed that every room should be searched immediately; another guest told how he had recently seen Mister creeping downstairs with a bundle under his outer clothing. Further to this, blood stains led from Mackereth's room directly to Mister's room! This was searched and after police found a bloodstained shirt and handkerchief, Mister was arrested on suspicion of attempted murder.

Within a short time it was ascertained that Mister actually had a room in Birmingham, but was seldom there, indicating that he was of the vagrant community. A constable was sent to Birmingham to search his room where he located a set of black-handled cut-throat razors, one of which was missing; these matched exactly the bloodstained weapon found in Ludlow.

It was a marvellous piece of police detection, resulting in the successful conviction of a brutal attacker and Mister was sentenced to death. William Mackereth was fortunate to survive the attack but he bore the horrific scars across his face and neck for the rest of his life.

Just one year later in 1841, a foul murder occurred at Bronygarth on the north western boundary of the county, to the north of Oswestry. The village of Bronygarth was a pleasant little environment, industrious and unassuming in character and size. Everyone knew everyone else and routines were adhered to.

Emma Evans was a local shopkeeper in the village; her shop doors were always closed and secured from the inside as casual browsers were not welcome. Her trade was regular and everyone in the area knew to knock on her door for access into the shop premises.

On a cold and dark December evening, Emma Evans heard a knock at the shop door; this was not unusual as she would serve until late at night. Emma opened the door and saw two men outside, these were to be her last ever customers. She admitted the men into the shop, but once within they turned violent. Emma was knocked to the floor as they frantically searched for money about her person and in other rooms. Emma lay whimpering like a tiny puppy who knows it has done wrong; her whining agitated the men who beat her with a poker until her head was a mass of pulp and virtually unrecognisable. They then stole some of Emma's personal property, silver, clothing and money before making their escape into North Wales.

Once there they made their way to the Kings Head at Cefn Mawr where their actions were more than a little suspicious. The pair were seen to drop a bundle outside the premises, strategically positioned so it could be collected on their way out. A member of staff noticed this and stepped outside to examine the bundle and saw the ill-gotten gains of their murderous deeds, though obviously he did not recognise these as such.

A short time later the pair left the Kings Head only to find themselves followed by two members of staff who had decided that the men were up to no good. During the chase the pair ditched the bundle and fled into the darkness. Meanwhile Emma Evans's body was discovered at Bronygarth and the Shropshire Constabulary called to attend, a local surgeon pronounced life extinct and enquiries commenced.

Several local people recalled seeing the two strangers in the locality; the men were identified as John Williams and William Slawson from Wrexham, well-known crooks and confidence tricksters. The various sightings of the two placed them at the scene at the approximate time of death, making them the chief suspects. Their descriptions and movements were circulated to all borough and surrounding forces as the two were clearly regarded as very dangerous men.

The bundle containing much of the stolen property was recovered and identified as belonging to the late Emma Evans; once again the descriptions of the two men seen with this at the Kings Head matched those of the men wanted for murder.

It was only a matter of time before Williams and Slawson surfaced elsewhere, and sure enough, two weeks after the murder they were found in Coventry attempting to sell some of the silverware with which they had successfully escaped. The police were notified and the men arrested; further items of cutlery bore the stamp E.E., a clear indication that these once belonged to Emma Evans. The two villains who were confirmed as Williams and Slawson were conveyed to Shrewsbury where they were tried.

Amazingly, Slawson was convicted only of robbery and sentenced to seven years' transportation, Williams for murder and sentenced to hang. There was public outrage as no one, including Williams, could believe that Slawson should escape the death penalty. The verdict seemed without logic, as it was Slawson who had delivered the first blow which knocked Emma Evans to the ground! His defence counsel claimed that he had intended to rob but not to kill; it had been Williams who attacked the defenceless woman with a poker, not Slawson.

Detective work during this era was in its infancy, yet as we can see, the constables dealing with serious offences were using their skills to determine the motives and identity of the offenders. Such actions laid a solid foundation for the future of policing throughout the world.

With the whole of Shropshire in uproar following the paltry sentence issued to William Slawson for his part in the Bronygarth murder the last thing law and order needed was a further contentious case. Yet just when matters were again returning to a semblance of normality a further outrage occurred.

Diana Biggs was sleeping soundly in her bed in the village of Stokesay late on February night in 1842, when she was awakened by a heavy knock at the door. It was a local cowman John Jones calling to ask for a drink. With what appears like incredible foolishness, Diana allowed him in to her home in order to quench his thirst.

Once within, Jones turned into an evil monster. He demanded sex with Diana and threatened to kill her children if they dare try intervene. Jones locked the doors to prevent anyone from within escaping and climbed into bed with Diana. Meanwhile the terrified children were made to stand and watch their mother so disgustingly degraded. It was a horrific scene, and one which still arouses a great deal of emotion at the mere thought.

As Diana Biggs screamed for mercy Jones produced a knife and plunged it several times deep into the struggling woman's chest. The onlooking children screamed as the frenzied attacker desperately tried to force himself on their brave mother, who was refusing him and fighting for her life.

One of the children slipped out of the room and managed to get out of the cottage and raise the alarm at a neighbour's house. Meanwhile Jones was rampant and refused to concede defeat. Diana Biggs managed to prevent further harm being done to her by gripping the sharp blade of the knife in her hand and forcing it away from her body. Blood oozed from the gash in her palms, but there was no pain, just fear. The pain would come later, much later when the matter was over, providing of course she lived through it.

Suddenly, it dawned upon Jones that one of the children had escaped, and realising that he was in deep trouble he quickly dressed and fled. There was but a few minutes between his flight and the arrival of the neighbour. The police were called to the scene and a surgeon treated Mrs Biggs' awful wounds. So far as detection goes, this was a reasonably straightforward case. John Jones was the offender and there was a desperate need to apprehend him.

With this in mind Superintendent Lewis pursued him and having trekked halfway round the county finally located him in Pontypool, Wales. Jones was traced to a local mine; local residents had seen a stranger acting suspiciously around there and duly informed the authorities. Lewis obtained the services of 15 constables and surrounded the whole of the mine area. There seemed no chance of Jones slipping through the tight security net. Minutes passed and a thorough search was carried out, but the elusive Jones was not there, once again he had escaped.

Within a few days he was successfully captured in Dudley and returned to Shrewsbury for trial. He was tried on charges of attempted murder and rape; he openly confessed to the latter charge but vehemently denied any allegation of attempted murder, claiming as his defence that the knife must have fallen out of his pocket!

He was found guilty on both counts and sentenced to 15 years' transportation. Superintendent Lewis was allowed £3 for his expenses in tracking down the criminal! Once again the courts dished out a sentence which did not appear to fit the crime. Mrs Biggs' life was virtually destroyed by the callousness of John Jones, her children would never truly forget the images of pain and degradation, and the unity of a whole family had been shattered.

The three cases in question depict different policing styles: of the skills displayed there is perseverance, dedication, commitment, investigative skill and communications with victims, witnesses, and other forces.

The Shropshire Force was formed into six separate sub-divisions county wide, with six superintendents being appointed by the new chief constable, and a further 31 constables being sworn in. Though a larger number had applied for the position, the majority were found to be unsuitable, some were actually criminals. After just one year, 18 of the 31 officers had resigned or left the force, 13 were sacked for committing criminal offences or for blatant neglect of duty, the most popular infringement being drunk on duty. This curious fact related to all police forces in England and Wales during the same era, a constable and alcohol was a cocktail for disaster!

January 1843 saw a new, more obvious danger to the officer pounding the beat in the towns and villages of Shropshire, that of physical assault, and once again Superintendent Lewis was involved.

A serious burglary having taken place, Lewis instructed Constable Jeremiah Smith to carry out enquiries. Smith identified a suspect, Richard Freeman of Upton Magna. A warrant was obtained and Smith and Benjamin Burgwin, the injured party, visited Freeman's home in order to execute the warrant and carry out a thorough search of the premises for Burgwin's stolen tools.

On arrival there Smith arrested Freeman on suspicion of burglary. Freeman was infuriated at the allegations and struck out at the constable, a fight ensued but after order had been restored, Freeman invited Constable Smith into his home to search for the property and thus resolve the matter. However, upon entering the house Freeman picked up an axe. Smith maintained a firm grip upon his collar, refusing to allow his prisoner to escape. Freeman aimed the axe at Smith's head several times in a determined effort to kill the officer. Jeremiah Smith fell to the floor, stunned by the initial blow; Freeman was bent over him and was about to cause more injury when Burgwin entered the house, carrying a large stick which he swung menacingly at Freeman, narrowly missing him. Freeman then left the injured officer and bolted from the house. Burgwin tended Smith who amazingly made a rapid recovery and carried out a search of the premises, repossessing much of the stolen property before making his way to Upton Magna for medical attention.

Freeman of course was still on the run, but his days of freedom were numbered and he was apprehended almost accidentally the following day when two gamekeepers found him hiding in some woodland. Freeman threatened them with his knife but found his threat ignored as the hefty gamekeepers knocked him to the ground and took him to the police at Wem, mistakenly believing him to be a poacher. In custody Freeman refused to co-operate with the police and would provide no personal details. However, a description was forwarded to Shrewsbury where he was quickly identified as the wanted criminal. Freeman was escorted back to Shrewsbury where he was tried and sentenced to a term of 20 years' transportation.

This was the first serious assault against a policeman with any form of media coverage in the county; presumably this displayed just how respected the constable's uniform and powers were becoming, as prior to this incident physical assault was a danger that all officers were expected to face. Sadly, the situation was to deteriorate before any significant improvement was achieved.

On the 2nd day of January 1849 Police Constable John Micklewright was killed on duty at Acton Burnell. His killer was Charles Colley, a rough and violent man who battered the constable to death during the execution of a crime. Colley attempted to prove that his actions were not deliberate and that he had no idea that Micklewright was a police officer attempting to arrest him; his actions had been defensive. The jury agreed on manslaughter and the judge sentenced Colley to ten years' transportation. A disgraceful verdict and sentence, for such a vicious crime the sentence should have been brought against a charge of murder! Thankfully, Micklewright is the sole officer in the Shropshire Constabulary to have been killed during the execution of his duty.

In 1850, the Bridgnorth force amalgamated with the Shropshire Constabulary. There was outrage at Bridgnorth when the Shropshire Chief Constable, Captain Mayne refused entry into the force of the Bridgnorth Chief Constable who was practically illiterate and devoid of any academic skills. The Bridgnorth officers denounced the decision and refused to transfer over; meetings were held with local councils and eventually it was decided to abandon the amalgamation as the Bridgnorth force had resolved to support their own Chief Constable; if he was refused entry then they would not go either! It was an impossible and almost ludicrous situation, which was eventually resolved some six months later by the Bridgnorth Chief being presented with an independent position.

Elsewhere independence was very much in evidence as the borough forces throughout the country maintained a separate image from their county counterparts, despite the political wranglings of the various local councils and politicians. Meanwhile illegal activities continued to occur at an alarming rate.

Few murderers receive any public sympathy, yet in 1857 a Shropshire killer actually escaped execution for an act of violent murder committed in Much Wenlock, on what is now the A458 between Shrewsbury and Bridgnorth.

Ann Evans was best described as 'different'; in the 19th century the people of Much Wenlock and surrounding villages knew her as a witch, a despicable woman with much malevolence in her heart. The people of Shropshire believed that Evans cast spells against their property or against them as individuals, for this she was shunned and every time livestock died, Ann Evans was blamed. It was unfortunate, but she did very little to rid herself of her evil reputation.

It came as something of a surprise when she introduced a local man, William Davies, into her life. Davies lived with Evans as man and wife, the common belief at the time was that she had him under a spell! Nothing was further from the truth. Aged just 35, Davies was his own man, with his own principles and chose to ignore local gossip about his common-law wife. Admittedly it was an odd relationship, as she was over twice his age and had seemingly little in her favour.

On 12th September 1857, for some reason William Davies apparently tired of the relationship and stabbed Ann Evans to death in the kitchen of her cottage. When he was brought to trial the court heard how Evans was a despised member of local society; there was not a single individual to say anything in her favour. All witnesses called to give evidence expressed sympathy for Davies.

The judge found him guilty but elected to ignore the death penalty due to the extenuating circumstances which had been discussed in court. A popular verdict at the time, but whether it was just and humane is another matter. Murder is murder; Ann Evans was an elderly woman whereas Davies was a young fit man.

Two years later, the Shropshire Constabulary Chief Constable, Captain Dawson Mayne tendered his resignation from the post. He had worked hard at presenting a good image and building for the future of the force, and although many of his decisions were unpopular, he was a good officer well respected by all who knew him.

Almost 100 applications were received for the vacant post of Chief Constable, from which Captain Phillip Henry Crampton, Irish born Deputy Chief Constable of the Somerset Force was selected. Crampton was a man of a similar vein to his predecessor, but with far more experience and he changed the force, introducing better administrative procedures which greatly assisted his subordinate officers. Crampton held the position for five years before resigning in July 1864, his replacement was Lieutenant-Colonel Edward Burgoyne Cureton.

Cureton was unfortunate during his very short tenure, for local civil riots caused a great deal of disturbance in almost every reasonably sized town in the county. Police officers found themselves suffering the brunt of public unrest during local elections, when many were assaulted with bricks, wooden batons, stones or anything that was handy. Reinforcements, of which there were few, were drafted in on trains, until eventually it was simply a one sided vendetta against the police who were alarmingly outnumbered. Remarkably no officer was ever killed during such riots. Cureton found it incomprehensible that the police could mount no retaliatory action against the mob, his ideas were of no use in a police environment and so he resigned in January 1866.

The next Chief Constable was Colonel Richard John Edgell from Essex. Edgell was a good leader of men and more than anyone he allowed the force to grow, and he nurtured in every one of its members pride in the uniform and an awareness of the responsibility such a position holds. One incident which typified his enthusiasm for the job and the support of his men occurred within twelve months of his taking office. Rioting was still endemic throughout the United Kingdom as politics took a greater role in the lives of ordinary people. Differences in aspirations and social background ensured widely divergent demands of economic policies. It was simply a case of rich against poor, with the latter treating the unfortunate police as whipping boys for the affluent class; they were an ideal target for violence.

The riots occurred with alarming frequency all over the county, and on a cold December night in 1867 the town of Wellington erupted into a frenzy of political violence. Telegrams were sent requesting back-up officers to attend at Wellington and at the various other locations throughout the county, but as all resources had been allocated, no one was available to assist at Wellington, where just 17 officers fought a running battle with the unruly mob, reckoned to comprise some two to three hundred folk!

With no resources available, Edgell went to the town himself and was horrified by the overwhelming force of numbers facing the police. He withdrew the officers, four of whom had been injured, to the sanctuary of the local police station and ordered them to remain there until such time as the crowds had dispersed and focused their attentions elsewhere. As anticipated the mob, whose violence had robbed them of any rational thought, duly dispersed.

By 1879 the County force had a complement of just 137 officers, and the local borough forces possessed anything from four to 25 officers dependent upon the size of the town. From such figures it is easy to see just how undermanned the independent police forces were. With the development of the police force one major factor had been virtually ignored, that of adequate payment for the constables whose wages were paltry and by no means in keeping with the physical stamina required and the dangers they faced.

The year 1887 saw the introduction of eight separate sub-divisions within the county force, at Shrewsbury, Oswestry, Whitchurch, Wellington, Bridgnorth, Church Stretton, Pontesbury and Burford, each of which was overseen by an officer of the rank of superintendent. Slowly but surely a rank structure was evolving and with it the expansion of the force, which between 1879 and 1888 recruited almost 150 further officers, boosting its complement and assisting the constant battle against crime.

The Local Government Act of 1888 ensured the abolition of borough police forces in areas where the population was less than 10,000; in effect this left Shrewsbury as the only town in Shropshire independent of the county force, which incorporated the officers from the boroughs into their own ranks.

This was the same year that Jack the Ripper terrorised London's Whitechapel, and there is now the possibility that the killer was in fact a resident of Shropshire before and after the crimes occurred. A police and crime historian friend has established during more than 35 years of research that the killer may have been a man who was employed in London and resided in the Whitechapel district in a position allowing him access to the murder sites and providing cover to disguise his crimes. According to the research the man was a serving police officer in London who had lost members of his family in a fire in the metropolis some years earlier. Those who knew him suspected him of killing his wife and family by deliberate arson, incensed by the thought of his wife's unfaithfulness with several other men. The man concerned, whom I am unable to identify, lived for some time in Shrewsbury, and similarly patterned sexual offences occurred in and around the county during his residence there, further, they ceased when he left the community only to recommence elsewhere. Finally upon his return to the county there is unique new evidence which indicates that Metropolitan Police senior officers were regarding certain members of their force with some suspicion. Inspector Abberline and Detective Sergeant Rolf visited Shropshire in the company of Dr Thomas Dutton, author of the *Chronicles of Crime*, self-proclaimed criminologist and personal friend of Abberline. They carried out enquiries into a suspect they had under observation at the time, indicating that there may be more than a possibility that the killer was from Shropshire. Certainly, if the research is ever published in book form, it will astound the so-called experts who dictate the thinking in the odd world of 'Ripperology'. I personally feel that this research is undoubtedly the most thorough yet undertaken and supported by evidence never previously thought available!

Whether Colonel Richard Edgell, the Chief Constable of Shropshire, ever knew of the suspicions of his metropolitan counterparts shall never be known, as he too is believed to have taken the secret to his grave when he died of a heart attack on the 26th November 1889. He was a sad loss to the county force, but during his term of appointment, some 23 years, he proved beyond all doubt that he was one of the most able men ever to run the force. His short-term replacement was his Deputy Chief Constable, William Galliers.

In 1890 a new chief was appointed, again an ex-ranking officer in the British services. Captain George Charles Peere Williams-Freeman was a strict disciplinarian and one of his first acts was to introduce a more thorough and comprehensive set of disciplinary rules for members of the force. He also changed the style and colour of the uniform, closer to the blue now associated with the police.

Williams-Freeman introduced first-aid training into the force curriculum and all those officers who qualified were to wear St John's Ambulance Association badges on the sleeves of their uniform. He also introduced a merit award, where again a badge was to be worn by the officers receiving such an award. What was more appealing to the officers within the force was the reward that accompanied the 'Merit' as each officer receiving the award, which was for a short period only, received an extra 'tuppence' a day.

Williams-Freeman was, despite his strict disciplinary beliefs, a senior officer who supported his men and fought to provide them with the best of everything, albeit some of the things that had not initially seemed sensible were in the long term of great benefit, such as the Constabulary Sports, which allowed his officers to socialise in a united fashion. The sports were a great spectacle covering a range of athletic events and very often attracted large crowds; more importantly, they created a new image of the police, enabling the general public to see the human side of police officers, most of whom were viewed as some form of moronic clone, created to be awkward!

The reality was of course totally the reverse. Police officers are only human, they too have emotions and opinions, they laugh, cry and worry like everyone else, indeed the tears flow a lot more often than most people ever realise, especially behind the walled sanctuary of the respective police stations. The emotional effects of dealing with death, despair and destruction can all too often boil over, escape from the forced cool exterior. This is one aspect of a police officer's life which has hardly altered in over 160 years. Our police are trained to deal with crime and the side issues which accompany it, counselling victims and putting them in touch with the various organisations which are there to assist them in times of crisis, yet at the end of each shift, who counsels the officer who has dealt with a dozen or more problems, each of them a crisis to the individual who has dealings with the police? Perhaps this is why the police officer is so often viewed as a different entity to the rest of society, because they are able to cope and have no emotions, but look beneath the uniform and you will see a mere human being.

Into the 20th century

After the death of Williams-Freeman, the post of Chief Constable of Shropshire Constabulary was officially advertised and 164 applications were received by the Salop Standing Joint Committee. Finally on the 1st March 1906 Major Llewelyn William Atcherley was selected. Atcherley had been a member of the East Lancashire Regiment since 1890, he was promoted to Captain in 1898 and to full Major in 1905 prior to retiring from the services in 1906.

The reign of the new Chief Constable saw the introduction of photographic equipment at the county headquarters, and a centralised office for the checking of habitual offenders was created at Scotland Yard, the fountainhead of all England's police forces. Here fingerprints and photographs of offenders could be registered and referred to by other forces if thought applicable to the crimes occurring in their areas. It was a marvellous innovation for the future of policing, making the detection of offenders so much easier.

Within two years of accepting his position, Atcherley left Shropshire in favour of northern territories and the West Riding of Yorkshire Force where he was appointed chief constable, presumably on vastly improved terms. Atcherley achieved very little during his short term in the force, perhaps his concept of policing was not what was required in rural Shropshire.

Within eight weeks a new Chief had been appointed. Captain Gerald Lysley Derriman took the helm on 2nd September 1908. Like so many of his contemporaries during the same era, Derriman was up against severe political administrative difficulties as he attempted to bolster the force's complement and increase manpower on the streets. To some small extent he was successful in this area, but other more serious matters were looming.

In August 1914 war was declared against Germany. Derriman could not resist the temptation of serious involvement in battle and applied to rejoin his old regiment, an application which was approved and on the last day of 1914 he left the force. Whether it was his overall lack of leadership qualities or perhaps a basic lack of interest in police work in general, but the force's morale dropped during Derriman's time as Chief Constable, and the crime rate soared as officers lacked the enthusiasm which had been instilled by previous senior officers. Derriman's departure was welcomed by many officers, yet when news filtered through to Shropshire on the 7th August 1915, that Derriman had been killed in action he received the greatest sympathy any man could wish from his ex-colleagues.

An honorary Chief Constable was appointed in the form of a Justice of the Peace, Mr Augustus Wood-Acton, who was very little more than a stop-gap. The activities overseas outweighed the importance of law and order in England. Wood-Acton died in 1918 and after the brief temporary appointment of Chief Superintendent Edge, a new Chief was appointed; Major Jack Becke took over on the 1st of July 1918. Seldom can a man have been faced with such a dilemma as he: police pay had failed to keep up with the cost of living, officers of the Metropolitan Force in London rallied the support of their colleagues nationwide for a strike and eventually around five to six thousand Metropolitan officers came out, causing absolute mayhem in the nation's capital.

Becke issued many supportive orders and instructions to his officers, and it was this support which perhaps remedied the situation in Shropshire, and he also negotiated a new pay scale backdated to the April of that same year which increased officers' salaries to a reasonable standard. Leave allowances were further enhanced and matters generally improved.

Becke introduced motor patrols into policing practice; the first of such patrols took to the streets of the county in December 1930 and Becke was hailed as a marvellous leader by every member of his force. Always one step ahead he continued to search for ways of improving policing methods and easing the job of his officers. The motor car greatly improved this, speeding motorists could be more easily apprehended instead of the old system whereby an officer would fake a speed trap by making himself visible to the passing motorist, in such a manner that it would seem that he was attempting to hide, being part of a speed trap. The motorist would slow down and thus become more accessible to officers on the beat!

Major Becke resigned from the force in September 1935, having been awarded the OBE in recognition of his excellent loyalty and quality of service. He then took the Chief Constable's post in

Cheshire. Captain Harold Arthur Golden replaced him and duly attempted to stamp his authority upon the force, reissuing orders and generally trying to tidy up administrative procedures to his own liking.

Golden was faced with an embarrassing situation in the form of Tony Hall, an ex-police inspector who proclaimed himself by blood the rightful heir to the throne of England. Hall was obsessed with this belief and made himself a public nuisance as he toured the area speaking about his beliefs and his self-proclaimed right to the throne. Despite this he was harmless enough and was dealt with in the same way as any other person of similar persuasion, albeit there must have been some relief when he finally died in 1947. Hall was not a true lunatic or a fool by anyone's standards, his knowledge of the law and his intelligence were excellent; but his obsession had overpowered his logic.

In August 1937 Constable Henry Speake tragically died in the river Severn pursuing three boys who had escaped from a local youth centre. It was later discovered that Speake, aged just 21, had suffered a heart attack through the shock of the cold water.

With the Second World War looming, Captain Golden resigned from his position; no immediate replacement was sought and the post was held by Superintendent Barnwell. Golden later went on to become the Chief Constable of Wiltshire.

In 1946, the first choice as replacement Chief Constable failed a medical, hence the appointment of Douglas Ormond of the Metropolitan Police. His era saw the introduction of the Police Act, and the abolition of the final borough force in the county of Shropshire. The Shrewsbury borough force amalgamated with the Shropshire Constabulary, and at last the county of Shropshire was being policed by one united force, the amalgamation taking place on 31st March 1947.

In July 1954 Shropshire Constabulary introduced a further aid in their fight against crime, police dogs, which were becoming fashionable and proving their worth elsewhere in the world. Ormond knew the value of having a force dog section and supported it as best he could. It gained a marvellous reputation with other forces throughout the United Kingdom, some of whom used it as a role model. Douglas Ormond resigned from his position in 1962, being replaced by Robert George Fenwick who up until that time had been Assistant Chief Constable of the Gloucestershire force, a man with an excellent reputation and who was ideally suited to taking the force forward. Finally on the 1st October 1967, officers from Shropshire became amalgamated with colleagues of the Herefordshire and Worcestershire Forces, so becoming more cost effective and efficient in administration and manpower. The independent force became the West Mercia Constabulary. Perhaps the personal touch of individual counties possessing their own police forces has been lost, but the professionalism and dedication of the officers patrolling the streets has not.

2

THE MURDER TEAM

The act of murder is often the ultimate step forced upon one human being by circumstances, or a sudden change in circumstances, arousing deep emotional distress, causing someone who can usually be described as 'perfectly normal' to slay another. I say perfectly normal, but who are we as individuals to assess just what is 'normal' and what isn't! However, one fact we can be certain of is that acts of violence and premeditated murder are not normal.

The majority of us can never imagine what it would be like to destroy another human being, to end an often perfectly innocent life with a deliberate action. Note that I say deliberate, and not accidental, for all too often killers attempt to detract from their obnoxious actions by faking mental disorder; some are so cunning as to attempt to arrange the crime scene to make it appear an innocent affair, nothing more than an unfortunate accident.

Thankfully, with the technology and knowledge which have been advanced and gained during the 20th century, deliberate acts of murder are none too easily suppressed. Crime scenes are meticulously examined by expert scientists who have an array of back-up resources available to them, ranging from chemical tests of blood or personal samples, to fingerprint testing, and minute clothing sample analysis. These individuals are known as Scene of Crime Officers, more commonly referred to as 'SOCO'.

SOCO have the potential back-up of eight official forensic science laboratories, spread throughout the United Kingdom, including Aldermaston and Porton Down, whose resources are available to investigating authorities. The evidence such research and scientific testing can produce borders on the miraculous and is a vital tool available to the police in their unrelenting fight against crime. It is essential that all agencies work together during a criminal investigation; and it is a team effort with each department playing a role. Strict principles must be maintained and adhered to, otherwise evidence may be lost or open to exploitation and ultimately rejected in a court of law. The case against the offender, no matter how obvious his guilt, must be watertight with no room for ambiguity or error, hence regular communication is paramount.

Crime and acts of murder have all too frequently been over-dramatised by the pen or typewriter of crime writers, the majority of whom have no physical or practical experience in the investigation of crime. There are too many writers upon the subject of murderous acts who proclaim themselves to be 'experts'! For example, the Victorian crimes of Jack the Ripper who slaughtered four common prostitutes in Whitechapel, London. It is an impossible task to identify this killer, yet there are those who proclaim themselves as 'experts' upon the case; what chance have such amateurs some 106 years after the crimes? The professional police force, complete with detectives armed with all the information and evidence available, as well as physical contact with their suspects, failed to track him down at the time of the murders, yet here we are, one century later with amateur detectives telling us that they have the solution! Such matters have to be put into some perspective, we will never solve the riddle of the identity of the Ripper; all that can be offered are feasible explanations.

Matters in 1888 would of course have been greatly improved had the Metropolitan Police, or even the Shropshire force, had the availability of forensic science; many more criminals would have been caught and punished, more murderers would have been convicted and thus the possibility of detection would have deterred many would-be criminals, and fewer crimes might have been committed. That is not to say that there would have been fewer murders for such a serious course of action is often involuntary or unpremeditated and thus inevitable no matter what the deterrent.

Shropshire has had its fair share of murders, especially so in the years leading to the 20th century, when many were of the unpredictable and unsolved kind. If only forensic science had been available to the officers dealing with the sickeningly callous murder of Elisabeth Preece in Pontesbury, which is located on the now busy A488 road to the south east of Shrewsbury. Today it is easily accessible, but in 1845 it was just the opposite; virtually remote, it was a self-reliant village.

Elisabeth Preece was a single parent residing in the community, not your average village resident, but best described as a young woman of loose morals. Elisabeth was mother to two bastard children with a third on its way. She could hardly be described as an astute sort of woman, but was more than capable of providing for her family, albeit in somewhat unethical circumstances. Elisabeth refused to discuss the identity of the father of the child she was carrying, except that he was financially secure and was going to allow her two shillings a week to support the family!

One Saturday evening in July 1845, Elisabeth disappeared from the face of the earth. She was last sighted in the early evening, alone, and going to post a letter at nearby Pontesford. Her family, alerted by her absence after dark, reported her missing, but as it was decided that she may well have been with a 'friend', there was no immediate panic.

The following day, a Sunday, a local worker found the bludgeoned body of Elisabeth Preece in a coal pit just outside Pontesbury. Her head had been so badly beaten as to make it difficult to recognise her; she was partially naked, some of her clothing was found in the coal-pit cabin, the rest was strewn around the crime scene.

Records do not show whether or not Elisabeth had been sexually abused, but it is a fair assumption. The police attended the scene and could do very little, many of the local villagers had visited the area, collected Elisabeth's clothing and touched the body. Police enquiries proved fruitless, apart from two young lads who claimed to have heard a female screaming in the area where the body was found.

An inquest was hurriedly opened, and quite amazingly, it was proffered that she may have committed suicide. The police objected to this opinion and insisted that it was murder. Despite every effort, no killer was ever brought to justice. The fact that Elisabeth was a woman devoid of principles ensured that the recollection of her death was somewhat short-lived, and the possibility that a mad killer was present within the confines of their small society was disregarded – perhaps the villagers of Pontesbury knew more than they would admit? It would seem that the killer must have been local, as the gates to the coal pit had been locked on the Saturday, yet the killer knew where the key was kept, and also knew of the pit's existence.

An earlier tragedy took place prior to the formation of a police force as we now know it. In 1822 law and order was very much a matter enjoyed by those who could afford to influence prosecution. Constables were elected by the gentry, indeed in some cases these positions were forced upon unfortunate members of a respectable community, who would be expected to house prisoners in their own homes and to stand guard over them 24 hours a day. Generally, they were the lesser members of society, unable to proffer any wealth to avert the position being forced upon them. It was very much a case of a social pecking order, with those at the bottom of the scale carrying out the menial tasks for the more affluent members of society.

However, as is always the case, there were those who naturally enjoyed the position of constable, which should not in any way be compared to the present day rank. The constable was a general dogsbody; more of an armed sentinel for the village or community, with no strict guidelines or job description. Basically, the job of constables was to prevent crime, at all costs, how they did this was left to their own judgement. In larger towns they were also lamplighters, some were men in their 70s or 80s, lightly armed with a cutlass or stick. Self-protection was the initial reaction, then to ask questions later, hence any suspicious characters lurking about communities at odd hours could find themselves clubbed before being questioned!

Constable Goodall was not such an officer; reasonably astute with an enquiring mind, he seems to have relished the role of constable. Goodall was called to attend the suspicious death of a baby in Bridgnorth in September of 1822. The child had been taken to a Dr Hall for urgent treatment, its mouth being blistered and badly burnt. Hall examined the baby and found traces of oil of vitriol (sulphuric acid) in its throat and mouth. As at this point the child was still alive he prescribed a magnesia solution as a remedy. Hall could not understand how the acid had been administered, surely such caring, loving parents as Mr and Mrs Richard Overfield appeared to be would not be so callous or careless as to deliberately or accidentally feed the child such a thing. The following day the child died, and Constable Goodall was called in.

A post-mortem was carried out on the child by Dr Hall; he confirmed that traces of sulphuric acid had been found in the child's digestive system and that this and its poisonous effects had been the cause of death.

When Constable Goodall visited the Overfield home he first talked to the child's father, Richard, who told him that the cat was to blame for on the day of the incident, he had knocked it from the slumbering child's face, where it had been sucking the infant's breath! Mrs Overfield was less informative, she stated that she had not witnessed the incident, but when her husband told her that the baby was in distress, she at once screamed out for help. As a result of this, a neighbour entered the house and found an acid smell to be present in the child's mouth. Having heard what Richard had said about the cat, she had tested the animal's mouth but found no such pungent smell.

Goodall spoke to several neighbours, most of whom described Richard Overfield as a hard-working and caring husband and father, never prone to acts of violence or rage. Goodall did not believe such statements, those who made them were simply acquaintances and not personal family friends or next door neighbours.

Eventually Goodall found a neighbour who told a different story. Louisa Davies often heard the couple quarrelling, and had seen Richard Overfield walking in the rear garden of their premises almost immediately after Mrs Overfield's initial cry for assistance. Louisa recalled seeing Richard stoop down at a spot in the garden. Sure enough, when a search of the premises was carried out, a glass phial was found lying close to where Overfield had been seen stooping down.

Constable Goodall had the phial, which contained a dark coloured liquid, examined. Needless to say, the liquid was identified as sulphuric acid. Richard Overfield was duly arrested by Goodall, tried and found guilty of murder and sentenced to death. It was revealed after the sentence that the child had been conceived prior to the couple's marriage. Richard Overfield had found it unbearable that he was to all intents and purposes forced into marrying his pregnant girlfriend, a fact which continued to cause him considerable grief, thus he rid himself of the child by murder. The efforts of Constable Goodall deserve some recognition, as undoubtedly this crime was solved by the use of expert evidence beyond the scope of the constable, but he utilised his resources extremely well, and perhaps created a precedent by associating forensic science with crime investigation.

The sensible and correct actions of the officer on the ground, be it a constable or higher rank, are of paramount importance. In modern day policing methods the first officer called to the scene of a crime must be alert to protecting the crime scene. On this officer's sole judgement depends the successful forensic examination of the scene. Within the space of a few seconds, the officer must assess the situation, decide upon a course of action, and abide by it. If necessary, assistance must be called to help with the security of the crime scene, especially that of a murder.

A cordon must be established, through which only the professional investigating authorities are allowed to pass; if the officer has touched anything then an exact note of this must be made, as well as of the route he took to the subject of the investigation: in the case of a murder, to the body!

As if that is not sufficient for the single officer at the scene of a murder to achieve, witness details must be obtained, as well as any other useful information which may be deemed necessary, such as who else has been close to the body, and why. Naturally, it is not in all cases feasible for the officer to follow such procedures, for crime scenes tend to be in the most unnatural environments. A room or a house would be easily cordoned off and protected, but what of public places, a busy thoroughfare, or a bus station where the scene has been contaminated by dozens of different persons? Security of the crime scene in such circumstances seems virtually impossible; however, as it still somehow must be attained, there are no real hard and fast rules as to how it should be done. It is dependent on the integrity and sensible approach of the first officer at the scene. Despite what some writers may claim, police training schools do not provide in-depth study of protection of crime scenes to their probationer constables; the subject is broached and seriously discussed, but the often unusual location of a crime scene makes it impossible to lay down rules. However, as the protection of real evidence is a less controversial topic, this is covered in some depth.

The police having arrived at the scene of a murder, within the space of a few minutes specialist organisations such as SOCO, forensic scientists, senior detective officers are all called to the scene; a police surgeon examines the body and pronounces death, the scene is measured and photographed again and again from all angles. Eventually the body is removed and the real investigation begins. Usually, whilst all this is going on, a murder incident room has been assembled; a focal point for all investigations into the crime. Every minute detail is recorded upon the Home Office Large Major Enquiry System (HOLMES) computer, operated and inputted by specialist staff, the majority of whom are police personnel, and within minutes the whole operation is up and running, deciphering the information it receives and utilising it to provide suitable options for its purpose. Statements, indexes, everything connected with the enquiry is stored within its complex memory; again, another vital tool in the fight against serious crime.

The microscopic scrutinisation of the scene continues, inch by inch and often takes days or weeks to complete, depending upon the evidence available. Whilst all this is going on, the police are out and about carrying out house to house enquiries, recording statements, speaking to other possible witnesses, in an attempt to identify a suspect or procure vital information. A murder investigation is often a laborious task, with countless enquiries being made, often over a huge area. It is a joint operation between specialist resources and investigating police officers. The technology available is without doubt an invaluable asset to the police; however, the majority of information used for such examinations or tests must be supplied by the police officer and all officers have a wide knowledge of the resources available to them and are expected to utilise these, no matter how large or small the enquiry.

The role of the everyday police officer seen on the streets of every town or city in the United Kingdom should never be underestimated. These officers have by necessity been made more adaptable to every type of incident they may encounter, from children playing football in the street, to being subjected to personal injury and physical assault, from being able to smile and display a relaxed homely attitude, to communicating news of a sudden death to a next of kin.

The police service throughout the United Kingdom has come in for a great deal of criticism; poor response times, failure to detect offenders, the increase in crime, the increase of deaths and accidents upon the highways of Britain – the list is endless, but nowhere in the world is there a more dedicated organisation than our British police forces. Ask any officer their opinion of the job and responsibility they hold, and there will be a virtually unanimous response; all are dedicated to the cause of fighting crime, all want to serve the public in the best way possible. It is no easy task. From one incident to another the role is variable and all too often volatile.

The police officer is not to be feared. The police are naturally inquisitive, but after all if they were not so then how many crimes would be successfully solved? This work displays the strengths and weaknesses of the human being; it is not the glamorised job depicted in the media but a sensible methodical approach, showing just how far police and scientific research into the study of crime has evolved since the beginning of the 20th century. I make no apology for my total support of every serving police officer in this country, all too often maligned, yet in a moment of crisis who do we contact? When in immediate danger who do we contact? When someone has forcibly entered our domain, be it a car or dwelling, who do we call? The answer to each of these is, the police. In truth, everybody's friend, but all too often portrayed as everybody's enemy!

3

A BUTCHER'S REVENGE

THE MURDER OF ELIZA BOWEN AT WESTBURY, NOVEMBER 1901

Severance of the carotid artery, or throat-cutting, as it is more commonly known, gained particular notoriety during the Victorian era, when Jack the Ripper slit his victims' throats with such ferocity as to almost sever the head from the body. Murder by this method is extremely messy, as the blood spurts from the wound, saturating everything within a close proximity. It is now an uncommon method of murder because there are other more convenient methods, less demanding of close physical contact and its risks.

The police and forensic team treat throat-cutting with great caution. For in common with all crime scenes, things are not always what they immediately seem. Imagine yourself on the scene of an incident where you have a body with a gaping neck wound, with a knife or blade nearby. Your first impression would be that this was murder; the victim's throat having been cut by the weapon. Yet people have committed suicide by this method, though it is hard to imagine the will-power such an act would take.

So where do the investigating authorities start? Obviously the incident scene is all-important. Then a certain amount of research into the dead person's background will provide information as to his or her state of mind. Enquiries in the immediate neighbourhood may elicit information as to suspicious noises heard or strangers seen in the vicinity. All this information provides a basis for further investigation.

Yet acts of violence are seldom well-planned or professionally executed; more often than not they are spontaneous reactions to a particular situation, and frequently they are caused by an over-indulgence in alcohol.

The village of Westbury is located on the central western boundary of Shropshire, and is reached by B class roads, which although not carrying a great deal of through traffic, tend to this writer's eye, to spoil the olde worlde village image so often encountered in Shropshire. Despite this, Westbury is quite a charming place. It is also synonymous with a curious act of murder.

Richard 'Dicky' Wigley was the son of a respectable tradesman. He spent most of his adult life in the county town of Shrewsbury, his adolescent years had been spent learning the trade which he was to eventually take up, that of a butcher. His father had been a hard-working man who was in the unfortunate position of having a desperately sick wife. Mrs Wigley was not physically ill, but suffered from mental delusions which caused her and the rest of the family much grief. Family quarrels were a common feature, although somewhat one-sided affairs, as Richard's mother accused her husband of all kinds of cruel acts. The unfortunate Mrs Wigley had spent several periods in a lunatic asylum but was never cured.

Such a contentious family environment was anything but conducive to the satisfactory upbringing of a child; however, Richard appeared to follow in his father's footsteps and was hardworking and thoughtful. That is until he reached his early 40s, when for reasons which can never truly be known, he took to leading the life of a drunken womaniser. Wigley had regular girlfriends for whom he openly displayed affection. Having reached his 40s, he had already married and settled down into a seemingly respectable life style. The memory of his mother's insanity had long since drifted from his memory, for now he had his own responsibilities.

The relationship with his wife deteriorated as the years progressed. Wigley took to late nights of socialising in the village hostelries in Cound and surrounding districts, but more so in the exaggerated social environment of Shrewsbury or Wellington. Wigley was a womaniser and a heavy drinker, facts which came to his wife's attention and duly caused a split in their marriage. Richard Wigley moved out of the marital home and into lodgings, initially at Cross Houses, where he found employment as a butcher, and later, in Hill's Lane, Shrewsbury.

This rural environment was not the ideal setting for the realisation of a relationship, yet Wigley met and fell deeply in love with a young woman by the name of Eliza Mary Bowen, whom he knew from his days of drinking at the Lion pub in Westbury, and who now worked as a housekeeper for a farmer and wealthy landowner in Cound. Eliza would regularly visit the butcher's shop in Cross Houses where Wigley worked, and struck up conversations with him; eventually he

The Lion public house – venue for the butcher's revenge.

asked her out for a drink. Eliza was almost half Wigley's age, a fact which may have attracted him. It must have been a supreme compliment to his self-esteem that he could still attract younger women!

Eliza Bowen was born at Llanfair, an attractive young girl not really clued-up on the often devious life present outside her immediate working environment, in which hitherto she had been perfectly safe. Sexual promiscuity was something that did not exist in the thoughts of this sensible young woman; her upbringing had been strict, as one would expect from devoted parents who cared for their daughter's well-being, and were thrilled at her finding employment in Cound. Previously she had worked in a similar position in Westbury, but her job also required her to work in the Lion public house, which was owned by wealthy farmer William Vaughan. Eliza had enjoyed working there, but it was hard work and long hours – facts which never enamoured the role to her parents, hence their interest and intervention to find her a different post in Cound. We can never be

44

sure as to whether Eliza was totally happy with the change of roles, after all, a young woman in her mid-twenties does have a mind of her own, yet she appears to have accepted the move without a great deal of argument.

So matters progressed. Wigley and Bowen would spend a great deal of time together, some felt too much time. Wigley's employer publicly condemned the situation; after all Wigley was still officially married. However, Wigley attempted to refute such condemnation by claiming that his marriage was finished, there was no further matrimonial bonding, both led separate lives and resided under different roofs! No matter how hard Wigley attempted to convince the public, his arguments fell upon deaf ears; most of those who knew him classed him as a ruffian when in drink, a perception which Wigley was to find would work against him.

In August 1901, Eliza Bowen left Cound and returned to her original employment at the Lion public house in Westbury. Although the relationship with Wigley was still ongoing, there were distinct signs that Eliza was tiring of the butcher's attentions.

The outside pressures placed upon any relationship by society in general can be massive, none more so than in such small communities as Westbury, Cound and Cross Houses, even to a certain extent in a town such as Shrewsbury, where people are acquainted with each other's affairs, especially those of high profile characters who earn something of a reputation for themselves, be it positive or negative. Unfortunately, most of the comments and rumours prevalent about Richard Wigley were of a negative nature. Rumour and general chitchat tend to increase as more and more people become aware of the individual and his or her circumstances. There is very little anyone suffering such gossip can do to prevent this occurring, it is part of human nature. In 1901, the whole of Shrewsbury and its surrounding area was rife with gossip about the Wigley-Bowen relationship, verging on the scandalous.

Not unnaturally, certain people close to Eliza Bowen advised her of the damage her liaison with Wigley was causing her reputation; peer pressure is a great thing, and eventually Bowen was forced to concede that she was being foolish, and that she should terminate the relationship. Indeed, Wigley had visited her at work in the Lion pub in Westbury on less than a handful of occasions during her second tenure there when he received a personal letter from her, telling him not to visit her at the pub again and that she would next visit him in Shrewsbury when she could. It closed with a reminder: 'Be sure not to come here again'.

Wigley was enraged, there could be no misunderstanding the tone of the letter, quite clearly Eliza Bowen was ending the relationship. Wigley was on his own, no real friends, no family, and now, no girlfriend whom he could manipulate.

Early in the morning of Saturday the 30th November 1901, Richard Wigley left his Hill's Lane lodgings and set out determinedly upon a full day's drinking. Alcohol tended to confuse his mind, allowing his problems temporarily to subside, and he fell deep into oblivion as the liquor took control of his thoughts and actions. It was as though Wigley knew he would never again walk the streets of the county's towns and villages, for he sold the majority of his butcher's tools for two shillings and sixpence, money which allowed him to satiate his appetite for alcohol.

Wigley found himself making his way out to Westbury, on foot and bemused by the over-indulgence in alcohol. Eventually he reached Westbury and entered the Lion public house, where he confronted Eliza Bowen, who was horrified by his appearance there and his drunken state. Wigley gave no intimation of his intentions, and purchased more alcohol which was avidly consumed. He was strangely quiet, as though in deep contemplation, offering no acknowledgement of Eliza's presence.

After a while, the pub emptied, leaving just Richard Wigley, Eliza Bowen and a servant, Ellen Richards. Wigley seized this opportunity to approach Eliza and he followed her into a passage-way within the pub and embraced her. Eliza wanted none of it and screamed out for help. Ellen Richards rushed into the passage-way to see what was happening, and saw Wigley holding Eliza. The terrified girl told Ellen to run and get the police, upon which Wigley released his grip and allowed Eliza to walk away from him to the bar area, then towards the cellar. The young Ellen was totally confused by the situation and did not know what to do for the best.

Within a few seconds both Wigley and Bowen were again locked in an embrace. Wigley had grabbed hold of Eliza's arm and pushed her against a wall, both were upright and Eliza was screaming for assistance. Ellen Richards stood rooted to the spot in terror; what she then witnessed was to live with her for the rest of her life.

Restraining Eliza against the wall, Richard Wigley seized a clasp knife from his pocket, and in a rage sliced it across Eliza's exposed throat. Blood gushed from the wound, saturating Wigley and the surrounding area. Eliza Bowen fell to the floor, managing to crawl a few yards towards the door before bleeding to death within the space of a few minutes.

Ellen Richards fled past the body of her friend and screamed for help. The rural tranquillity of Westbury was devastated by the obvious terror in her voice. Within seconds, men from the village arrived at the scene and saw the dead body of Eliza Bowen lying within the front door of the public house. They could hardly have had time to come to their senses when Richard Wigley emerged from the confines of the pub, clasp knife still in hand, and admitted that he had killed the woman. 'I have done it, lads. I have done it for love. I have come here on purpose to do this. I am ready to swing.'

Within a few minutes Police Superintendent Elcock arrived at the scene, and at once arrested Richard Wigley on suspicion of murder, and transported him to Shrewsbury, where he was questioned and openly confessed to murdering the young woman.

Several witnesses were interviewed in Shrewsbury, tracing Wigley's movements from leaving his lodgings, right through to his arrival at Westbury. Each and every public house he had called in en route was visited, and statements recorded from those with a pertinent story to tell, until piece by piece a complete picture was created of Wigley's last drunken binge. It transpired that Wigley had told several people in the various public houses of his intention to murder, most shrugged off such boastful claims as 'beer talk', none actually expected him to see it through.

His subsequent trial at the Shrewsbury Assizes was a straightforward affair. In his defence, Mr Bosanquet tried to claim that Wigley had inherited some of his mother's madness, and that he was in no fit state to be aware of the consequences of his actions. The prosecution refuted such preposterous suggestions, and offered solid evidence, provided by a thorough police investigation, complete with witness statements and a complete dossier upon Wigley's movements on the day in question. There was even an insight into the relationship between killer and victim. Such evidence is not easily refuted, and the defence knew they had very little chance of Wigley escaping the death sentence. Indeed, he was found guilty and sentenced to be executed, at Shrewsbury on the 18th March 1902. His executioner was Henry Pierrepoint of Manchester. Henry was the latest of the Pierrepoint family to serve as state executioner. He was assisted in this duty by John Ellis.

Richard Wigley may well have been the unfortunate victim of self-inflicted circumstances; his life was ruled by a craving for alcohol, which ultimately destroyed him and forced him to an early grave.

Although there was no question as to his guilt, the police provided every available scrap of evidence which may have proved necessary during the trial. Perhaps they were fortunate that so many people came forward to volunteer their statements; in all too many cases, innocent bystanders do not wish to get involved. However, the people of Shropshire were only too willing to assist in any way they could, and to rid their society of a brutal killer. This proves that the detection of crime is not simply a matter for the police, for without the assistance of the public the investigating authorities would all too often be unable to make progress. Long may the united approach remain.

4

ONLY THE STRONG SURVIVE

A CASE OF INFANTICIDE AT PETTON, FEBRUARY 1902

Of all the murders investigating police officers have to face, those involving young innocent children are more of a traumatic experience than those involving adults. Whether this is because the child victims are so hopelessly inadequate at defending themselves, all too naive for their own good, or whether those investigating immediately relate the victim with their own children and families can never be truly assessed. No matter which, it does affect officers who are involved with these investigations.

Such a horrendous crime occurred in the quaint little community of Petton in 1902, a crime which left an affluent society asking many questions of themselves and the restrictions they placed upon their domestic workforce.

Petton is situated in the north west corner of Shropshire, roughly midway between central Shrewsbury and Oswestry. It is by no means an ugly village, indeed by 20th century standards it has maintained some picturesque beauty. The murder which occurred here in 1902 was not the first dark secret of the parish; in March 1826 a frightful robbery took place upon the highway in Petton.

A gang of five highway robbers stopped a horse and gig and robbed its occupants, two men travelling from Wrexham to Shrewsbury. The attack was so intense that the robbers all but slit one man's throat, and the second man also suffered horrific wounds, sufficiently so as to warrant a charge of attempted murder against their attackers.

Just two weeks later the gang were apprehended in Manchester while attempting to sell some of their ill-gotten booty. It was ascertained that the five were part of a larger gang who had terrorised surrounding counties. Their arrest and confinement was deemed a marvellous coup, and released a great deal of pressure from the locality. Conveyed to Petton the five men were individually identified, brought to trial and subsequently executed.

Some 76 years later, the highway robbery was all but forgotten; the passage of time is a great healer of memories, be they good or bad. Perhaps the memory of the atrocity would have lingered, had either of the victims been inhabitants of Petton, but as they were all but strangers, the people of Petton classed it as an unfortunate incident.

Village life in 1902 was vastly dissimilar to its present day counterpart; today village life is based upon all things being equal. True, many villagers still rely on income from the land, either working for or owning farms. But there are equally as many who reside in a village environment purely for its tranquillity; during the normal working week they may commute to and from the larger towns or cities.

In 1902, however, things were vastly different. Families were born and raised in villages, and there they remained just as their ancestors had, often in the same cottage or house for many generations. All too often the housing was provided by the gentry, wealthy land owners who paid the people of the local village to be part of their workforce on the land.

One such landowner in 1902 was the Cooke family, Susannah and Lewis Cooke, who resided at Wackley Farm, Petton and employed a small number of local people as live-in house staff. In 1899 they took on Clara Elizabeth Lowndes, a 19 year old girl who seemed quietly pleasant, and keen to work for the family. Susannah Cooke enjoyed a friendly relationship with her employees, although strict household rules had to be adhered to, and she was not over-familiar with any of them. Similarly Lewis Cooke refrained from fraternising with his employees.

Although to the modern view this might appear to have been a strange environment, it should be remembered that attitudes were very different in 1902, and such things as social status were of primary importance.

Clara was a hard worker, her duties commenced at around 5 am when she would go down to the barn (milking shed) and milk some of the cows, thus ensuring fresh milk for the farm and part of the village. With this completed she would then carry out general farmyard duties, before retiring to the kitchen where she would be expected to cook breakfast, complete with freshly laid eggs, for her master and mistress.

Her reward for such arduous tasks was a paltry weekly wage, accommodation and food on the farm. Clara appeared to relish her role, and never complained. She received regular holidays when she could return home to her family and hopefully return, refreshed and keen to assist on the farm. The Cooke family knew very little about Clara's personal life, as she was sensibly discreet when it came to discussing such matters. For a servant girl to be sexually promiscuous or even rumoured to be so could lead to dismissal. The gentry saw such behaviour as something of a social stigma and would often rid themselves of staff whom they suspected of promiscuity.

In December 1901, Susannah Cooke noticed a change in Clara Lowndes' manner; and she appeared to be putting on a lot of extra weight. Susannah carefully broached the subject with Clara, but the servant denied the allegation. Susannah sent Clara home for her Christmas holidays, then wrote to her requesting her not to return to Wackley Farm if she was 'enceinte', not the most pleasant manner in which to address such a problem, but nonetheless, she had faced it, and believed that Wackley Farm would never see Clara Lowndes again.

To everyone's surprise, Clara returned to her position in late December 1902. Once again Susannah Cooke expressed her concern about Clara's size, but the servant still refused to admit that she was pregnant. Matters gradually deteriorated. Clara continued to rise at 5 am and maintained a high work rate in an attempt to disguise her condition.

By February she had slowed down, and was clearly unwell. Susannah Cooke attempted to force her to see a doctor but Clara refused. Then, on the morning of Monday 24 February 1902 Clara rose at her usual time. She fed milk to a few calves and returned to the house to prepare breakfast. Clara was unwell, she complained of a sharp pain in her right thigh and she found it difficult to stand up. A concerned Susannah gave her some pills and told her to go to bed and to remain there until she felt well enough to get up. Mr and Mrs Cooke were by now well aware that Clara was indeed pregnant.

A short while later, Susannah happened to glance over towards a farm outbuilding and was surprised to see Clara entering the outhouse. She also saw that Clara's smock was soaked in blood, and that blood covered her hands and part of her face as though it had been smeared. Clearly Clara was in great distress and when asked by her mistress if she had given birth, she vehemently denied it and claimed that the pills she had been given had made her mouth bleed. Susannah ushered her from the outhouse and back to her room, instructing her niece to ensure that she remained there.

With Clara out of the way, the suspicious Mrs Cooke returned to the outhouse. A brief look around the inside of the brick-built premises revealed all. Someone, presumably Clara, had attempted to hide the body of a new-born baby within the outhouse, all that was visible was the child's legs.

Shocked and presumably sickened, Mrs Cooke ran directly to Clara's room and confronted her with what she had seen. Clara pleaded with her mistress to remain silent over the affair and assured her that nothing would alter if she would only forget what she had seen.

Susannah sent immediately for the police, and within a short time Police Constables Rudge and Bolderston were at the scene, and commenced immediate enquiries. The first individual they sought out was Susannah Cooke. 'What has occurred here?' asked the curious officers. 'It's murder,' replied the lady of the farm. Having listened intently to what Susannah told them, and discovering the basic facts, the officers intensified their investigation. 'Did anyone witness the incident?' they asked, and were told 'No'. 'Was anyone else present in the outhouse when Mrs Cooke saw the suspect in there?' Once again they received a negative response. 'Do we know who the father of the child is?' Again the reply came as 'No'.

Both police officers then entered the outhouse, requesting that everyone else remain outside. There they found the corpse of a baby girl, partially concealed beneath some hay and other materials, leaving just its tiny feet and lower legs exposed. Tentatively, the officers removed the debris covering the infant's body, which was still covered in the bloody remnants of birth.

Closer inspection revealed that the child's mouth had been stuffed with paper, some of which protruded out of the mouth and covered the baby's nose and chin. Sensibly, neither Rudge nor Bolderston touched or attempted to remove the paper.

The two officers then requested that Dr Bathurst of Ellesmere attend the scene, which they duly preserved until his arrival. This was a simple precaution which enabled the doctor to pronounce life extinct, and to survey the immediate scene for himself. The child's body was removed to await a post-mortem examination, which took place two days later, the 26th of February.

Clara Lowndes was arrested on suspicion of the murder of her own child, now more aptly identified as infanticide. She was held in custody pending further investigations by the police. In the interim period, a case file was prepared from the facts obtained from the various witnesses at Wackley Farm.

When Dr Bathurst carried out his post-mortem examination he noted that it took a good pull to remove the first piece of paper from the child's throat, whoever had placed it in there had done so with considerable force, thus proving that this could not have been caused accidentally. A further piece of paper was found lodged in the back of the infant's throat, stuck to the oesophagus. Its lungs were of a bright red colour and as these showed no sign of disease, it was clear that the cause of death was due to asphyxia. The force used to cram the paper into the tiny orifice had been unusually vigorous and agitated, and bruising around the mouth further confirmed that the child had been roughly treated, and this a new-born infant.

Clara Lowndes spoke freely and openly to the investigating authorities; as she was extremely distressed and clearly in need of medical assistance she was placed under no pressure or duress. Her original plea for silence to Susannah Cooke tended to indicate an admission of guilt, but as so often happens, it was not a clear cut case of premeditated murder. It went much deeper than that: this was psychological despair, an involuntary reaction by a woman who ordinarily would act in a responsible manner. A hard-working young woman who strove to attain a reasonable standard of living for herself and who was, in the opinion of everyone who knew her 'conscientious and extremely pleasant'. The question asked by everyone at the time was, how could such a woman commit such a dastardly cruel act upon an innocent child; a new-born baby could hardly provoke its mother's anger or aggression.

Today, we know of the mental despair and pressures childbirth can create upon members of both sexes. Post-natal depression is a common enough symptom, and is recognised as a definite cause for concern. In 1902 such a syndrome would not have been officially recognised, yet this particular case set something of a precedent, as both prosecution and defence clearly understood the possibility of the mental anguish of a woman in Clara Lowndes' position.

The trial, held at the Shropshire Assizes, was never really a matter of life or death as far as Clara was concerned. A great many people had taken pity upon her. Character witnesses came forward, including her employer Susannah Cooke, who said that she would accept her back at Wackley Farm, if the opportunity ever arose; a greater compliment could not have been made, and was truly a magnanimous gesture.

It was perfectly clear that Clara was not mentally normal at the time she committed the crime, and no matter how much pity her predicament aroused, it should never be forgotten that she had indeed committed a serious criminal offence, that of taking another human life. The *mens rea* of the offence, namely, the guilty and blameable state of mind at the time of the offence, was clearly ambiguous. Clara could never have been adjudged in control of her own actions. Having just given birth, terrified that she might lose her employment on the farm, and thus any income necessary to raise a young child, she had acted in an irrational manner.

During his summing up of the case, the trial judge intimated that the maximum charge which Clara Lowndes should face was that of 'Concealment of Birth'. Clara was found guilty of that offence and was, after great deliberation, sentenced to six months' imprisonment. The 20th century legal system in Shropshire commenced with great integrity and common sense. The attitude and approach of Police Constables Rudge and Bolderston, their preserving of the crime scene, leaving it virtually untouched, thus allowing the doctor to utilise his specialist skills, and finally, the sensible attitude adopted during the subsequent trial. Seldom do the agencies of law and order attain the credit they deserve, this individual case warrants such praise.

5

DEATH OF A MARRIAGE

THE MURDER OF MRS JOHN DAVIES AT OSWESTRY, OCTOBER 1902

It is common knowledge that many murders are domestic affairs; the internal wranglings of a disintegrating relationship can cause violent scenes in what on the surface appears a reasonably happy household. Everyone at some time or other has had a disagreement with a partner; when living with another person there are bound to be times when things go wrong. Most of us can control our tempers; others lash out with verbal abuse, often with physical violence. If a weapon is used this can be an ordinary domestic implement, perhaps a knife. The most lethal type has a jagged dog-tooth edge which rips the flesh, making surgical repair of the wound all the more difficult.

Oswestry is situated in the north-west of Shropshire and is one of the county's major towns. It has a varied and somewhat chequered history; fire and battles have destroyed much of the old town, yet it is still a pleasant place, full of friendly folk and a thriving little market.

Mr and Mrs John Davies of Oswestry found their love and wedded bliss inextricably deteriorating as time went on. The longer they remained together the worse their relationship became. John Davies was a poultry dealer, having spent most of his life in markets and earning money by trading on the streets of Wales and the surrounding English border counties. In 1902, Davies was 70 years of age and had been married for some 36 years. The deterioration of the relationship may seem ridiculous, as one would expect that after such a lengthy period of living with one person every emotion and marital situation would have been encountered. Sadly in the case of Mr and Mrs John Davies, this was not so.

In the late 1890s and early 1900s John had taken to heavy drinking sessions, which were creating domestic disharmony in the form of violent rows about money being wasted on drink and lack of attention. So depressing did the situation get that Mrs Davies was forced to seek a separation order from her husband. It would seem that she had some good cause to stake this claim; when under the influence of drink John would regularly beat her and make irrational threats against her life.

The relationship broke down and John Davies moved into the Oswestry Workhouse where he remained for a few months before being discharged on the 6th October 1902. He was still selling poultry on the markets and so was presumed to be able to maintain a roof over his own head rather than be kept within the state workhouse.

After his discharge Davies set out for his old family home in Llys Lane, Oswestry, where his wife still resided, and by sheer coincidence he happened to meet her as she left the house. Davies tried to speak to his wife, but she made no reply and simply glared at him with a look of contempt; then stormed off in the opposite direction to her husband. A witness who happened to be in the area at the time of this incident later stated that John Davies had called his wife 'a bloody woman'.

Within seconds he was walking behind Mrs Davies and gaining on her with his large ungainly stride. Two men, Thomas Bromley and Thomas Owen, who were walking towards Llys Lane from Oswestry market via the railway met with the couple who by this stage were walking side by side. Mrs Davies had cried out for help and the two strangers had rushed to her assistance. John Davies explained that they were in fact man and wife and that all was well, it was simply a mild family quarrel.

The two men had no alternative but to accept this explanation; certainly the female did not look in too great distress, and so they nonchalantly proceeded on their way. It was to be a fatal mistake, as the pair had hardly left the quarrelling couple when they heard further distressed cries from the woman. Both men instinctively turned to see what was now occurring, and were mortified by what they witnessed. John Davies had removed a knife from his pocket and thrust it into the struggling woman's chest, she immediately ceased her struggles and flopped to the ground.

The two men ran to the woman's assistance, with Owen attempting to revive Mrs Davies and pull her to her feet, but it was too late, for although she managed to stand up she almost immediately collapsed and died on the spot. Whilst this was going on, John Davies attempted to cut his own throat, but was prevented by Thomas Owen who, realising that the woman was beyond help, flung himself at her attacker, knocking him to the ground. Davies was still armed with the knife and made several attempts to stab Owen, only to be overpowered with the assistance of a railway worker who came across the pair fighting. Davies was disarmed and forced to abandon any efforts to escape.

It took some considerable time for the situation to calm down, and when it did, John Davies was rambling that he had not stabbed his wife, she had scratched herself on a briar or root! He pleaded with his captors to let him die or to kill him.

Eventually, after the alarm had been raised, the police arrived, Superintendent Lewis and two constables, who immediately arrested Davies and took him to the local lock-up. There he was formally charged with murder to which he replied, 'I am sorry sir, I was forced to do it, she has ruined me.'

Further police enquiries revealed that Davies had premeditated the crime, having had the knife blade specially sharpened. Davies himself told the investigating officers that he had no money to purchase food or drink and had gone to ask his wife for mercy and for a small loan to bide him over for a week or so until he could repay her from working at the market. Mrs Davies, understandably, refused to give him any money and had told him to go away, hence the attack. Davies was later removed to Shrewsbury gaol to await trial.

The courtroom drama which so often accompanies cases of murder or other serious crime was little less than a farce on this occasion. John Davies was clearly an old man, but even worse, he was an old man who had lost his way. Medical evidence was produced stating that he found it difficult to sleep and was virtually an insomniac; his health was deteriorating and his life expectancy short. It was further alleged that he was incapable of making any rational judgement at the time of the crime, and was in fact, insane! With such powerful medical evidence, the prosecution had virtually no case to offer. Davies had already confessed to the crime, but pleaded insanity. There were many present who felt sorry for the silver-haired old man who stood trial for murder.

John Davies was found guilty of murder but was adjudged to have been insane at the time of the offence, so was therefore sentenced to imprisonment at Her Majesty's Pleasure.

Thirty-six years of marriage destroyed by a moment of madness, and an act of despair, or was it a cry for help? John Davies maintained his love for his wife, yet the years of alcohol abuse had deadened his feelings so that he was not the caring man she had married all those years ago. Just what the reason for this murder was – love, hate, jealousy, avarice – we shall never know.

6

THE CHURCH STRETTON AXE MURDERS

THE MURDER OF EDITH AND KATHLEEN DOUGHTY AT CHURCH STRETTON, OCTOBER 1924

Perhaps no other method of killing rouses more shuddering revulsion than the axe murder. Most of us, when hearing of someone being attacked by an axe, conjure up horrific scenes of mutilation and blood. Many such cases are doubtless drink related, and therefore unpremeditated. The murderer, his senses befuddled, seizes the first weapon to hand – usually a blunt instrument but on occasion an axe or machette – and lashes out at his victim for often the most trivial of causes. How often do we hear of an assailant, once apprehended, pleading guilty not of murder but of manslaughter through 'diminished responsibility'?

In a blunt instrument attack, forensic evidence can quickly identify from the wound the type of weapon used to inflict it; even the make or model. Where an axe has been used, the wound will obviously indicate that a blade-type weapon has caused it.

One could well be forgiven for believing axe murders to be few and far between in today's society. With so many easier methods available we think they should be quite rare, if not non-existent. Our perception of an axe-wielding murderer is generally very different from reality; we imagine such a killer as being a blood-crazed lunatic, lashing out with blood-stained axe at all and sundry. Few killers are typical of this image; they are generally domestic murderers, that is to say, those involved in family quarrels and confrontations; an axe, though less readily to hand than a kitchen knife, is sometimes available as a weapon.

The Lizzie Borden case is perhaps the most infamous axe killing recorded in criminal history. However, Shropshire has its own

The scene of the Church Stretton axe murders, 28 Sandford Avenue.

axe murder, equally as callous and cruel, but not as well publicised.

The affluent town of Church Stretton lies midway between Shrewsbury and Ludlow to the south of the county. It is the larger of three Strettons, the others being All Stretton to the north, and Little Stretton to the south. It is well known in geology circles, for it is situated in a valley which was believed to have been formed by two parallel faults, and the area in which the town lies is often referred to as 'the great Church Stretton fault'.

Hard working men in rural communities are common enough, indeed, I must include women in this category, for perhaps even more so in the 1920s than in the present day, families would work

59

together maintaining what was often a family run business. The local community would loyally support its local shopkeepers and suppliers of various provisions; it was a caring, sharing attitude which was not unknown to Church Stretton.

John Doughty was a typically conscientious resident of Church Stretton, working from his home above a shop at number 28 Sandford Avenue. Doughty had suffered greatly during the early 1900s when his wife was struck down by an illness which incapacitated her, thus requiring his devoted attention. This problem was exacerbated by the fact that he had a grocer's shop to run; not only was his family welfare reliant upon this, but also the well-being of the residents of Church Stretton. Doughty took in an assistant to help with his wife's everyday needs, thus allowing him to escape into his shop and earn a living. Mrs Doughty's suffering lasted for around ten years before she finally died, and although not the nicest thing to say, it must have been some relief for the loyal and devoted John Doughty, who was always there when needed.

Doughty gradually overcame the sad loss of his wife, and resumed his daily routine. He was a quiet unassuming man whose loss had evoked great sympathy in the Church Stretton community. Time is a great healer, and John Doughty began courting another local woman, by the name of Edith Waller, who was a district nurse. The couple were inseparable and appeared overwhelmingly happy. In 1919 they married, in 1921 their child Kathleen was born. John Doughty was thrilled with his daughter and spent every minute of his spare time with her.

Friday, the 24th October 1924 seemed like any other day in Church Stretton. The village shops were opening for business at an early hour, and many of the local residents were commencing their daily work. It was around nine o'clock in the morning when the first hint of disaster struck, and it was noticed that Doughty's grocer's shop was unusually late in opening.

Close by the shop was a café which was always busy during the first few hours of the morning, as travellers and local men refreshed themselves and women would call in as a break from their domestic chores. A small child playing to the rear of the café could hear odd groaning noises from the Doughty premises, the noises were not clearly distinguishable, but were obviously from someone in distress. The child ran into the café and alerted Harold Holmes, who ran to the front of the Doughty premises and found the main shop entrance door locked. Running back through the café, he entered the rear yard, which was separated from the Doughtys' by a six foot brick wall. Holmes scrambled over this, and was horrified to see John Doughty laid on the ground of the rear yard on his back in a semi-conscious state.

Holmes knelt over Doughty and could clearly see that the man was in considerable distress. Holmes (surely an apt name under the circumstances) looked around to see if he could ascertain what had happened. There was nothing for Doughty to trip or fall over, and even more suspicious was the fact that there was no trace of his wife Edith, or the child. Harold Holmes instinctively looked up from the spot where Doughty lay and saw an open window some 23 feet above. This was the only explanation for Doughty's predicament, he must have fallen from the window, yet there was still the mystery of the whereabouts of his wife and child.

Holmes hammered on the rear door of the building, which was locked from the inside. He made several attempts to raise the occupants, all to no avail. Panic set in as it suddenly dawned upon him that something was very wrong. It was an unfortunate position he found himself in, and those who had gathered on the other side of the dividing wall could never have imagined how Holmes felt. Controlling himself, he instructed someone to go and fetch the police, whilst he attempted to get into the premises.

A sudden rush of adrenalin surged through the unfortunate Holmes as he thought he heard a groaning sound from within the premises. He frantically searched around for a means of entry and located an insecure window, through which he climbed and commenced a search of the house.

Nobody deserved to witness the bloodshed which presented itself to Harold Holmes. Edith Doughty and the young child, Kathleen, had been brutally attacked and lay in the kitchen saturated in their own blood. There was little if anything which could be achieved for Edith and Kathleen, such was the extent of their injuries. Holmes ran out of the premises and passed on the information, making further demands that the police be notified immediately.

At 9.15 am Inspector Charles Henry Roberts arrived at the scene. John Doughty was conveyed to Church Stretton Infirmary for immediate treatment, he was the sole survivor of the horrors of 28 Sandford Avenue; both Edith and Kathleen were dead, victims of murder!

News of the atrocities quickly spread through the district and crowds gathered to the front and rear of the premises, newspaper reporters flocked to the scene from all over the county and the Midlands region in search of each and every horrific fact emanating from the house. Local people openly cried at the thought of how the victims had suffered; it was common knowledge that Edith and Kathleen were dead, and there were many who felt a great deal of sorrow for John Doughty, whose long-standing suffering was apparently now to continue. No man could carry such a burden. How would he react? Who could have done such a thing to so charming a family? Was their attacker local? These were all questions which buzzed through the congregated mass in Sandford Avenue.

Inside the murder house Inspector Roberts was in deep conversation with the shocked Harold Holmes, interviewing him about every detail he observed during his discovery. Roberts had already assessed the scene and noted that a wooden-handled axe was leaning against a chair in the blood-soaked kitchen; there was never any doubt that the axe was used in the commission of the murder. It soon became clear to the police that if the killer had been an outsider he or she would have found it difficult to make their escape; the front and rear doors of the premises were secured from the inside and the window through which Holmes had climbed was extremely stiff, making it most unlikely that a blood splattered killer would take the time to climb out through a small window and to close it again once outside! Furthermore, there were no obvious signs of disturbance within the house or shop area; nothing had seemingly been removed. Harold Holmes was a marvellous witness, he recalled everything he had seen and done and was of great assistance to the investigating authorities.

Meanwhile at the Church Stretton Infirmary John Doughty regained consciousness. His back injury was not as bad as first feared and although it was deemed serious enough to warrant his transference to the Royal Salop Infirmary it was not life-threatening. Police officers visited Doughty in hospital and events took a dramatic turn when it was realised that John Doughty's own clothes were in fact covered with blood. There was just one possible reason for this; he had been in the immediate vicinity when his wife and child were bludgeoned to death. Although the police did not wish to make a great deal of it while Doughty was still critically ill, eventually he would have to be arrested on suspicion of murder.

Edith and Kathleen were buried at Church Stretton with great expedience; there was little doubt that it was right to have them buried as quickly as possible in order to allow normal life to continue, thus their remains were interred on Tuesday 28th October 1924.

The following day, John Doughty was officially taken into police custody and charged with the unlawful murder of his wife and infant daughter. He denied all allegations and was obviously psychologically disturbed by everything occurring around him. His mental condition deteriorated until he was in such a state as to warrant him insane.

A search of the murder house located upwards of 100 unopened letters, some of which were unpaid bills and demands for payment for goods provided to Doughty. In all it was found that he had incurred debts in the region of £100 which, in today's financial terms would be a considerable sum in excess of £10,000! There was very little else of any evidential consequence within the premises.

House to house enquiries in the locality revealed little if anything which could explain why Doughty committed the murders. The couple were to all intents and purposes loyal and devoted, there were very few people who had anything sinister to say about the family, and those who did were believed to be ill-informed as no evidence of violence or quarrels was forthcoming from any other source. John Doughty eventually stood trial and was found guilty of murder, but was certified as insane and detained at His Majesty's Pleasure, thus escaping certain execution.

The police were almost completely at a loss as to a motive for the murders, the only explanation that could be found was that Doughty had been consumed by the worry of his mounting debts, the inability to provide for his family and the possible loss of self-respect within the community if such a matter should be publicly revealed. In a blind rage and in a mental state which was beyond his control, he had butchered his wife and daughter, thus ridding them of the stigma of being virtually bankrupt. With this achieved he then attempted to commit suicide by leaping out of an upper-floor window, but had failed. There is no doubt about his guilt, his mental condition was not compatible with his everyday actions and responsible attitude. His insanity must have been accelerated as he lay in the rear yard of 28 Sandford Avenue, albeit semi-conscious, but who knows what horrors passed through his subconscious in those fateful few minutes; the recollection of his actions would be enough to push anyone over the edge.

Murder is unforgiveable, I make no defence for any such act, but one has to have some sympathy for John Doughty. His life for over ten years had been one of drudgery and despair with his invalid first wife, followed by the mounting debts and lack of self-respect for failing his second wife. Having said that, there can only be revulsion for the cruel way in which he despatched his family from this earth. Self-destruction would have been a more suitable option for him, rather than destroying two further lives. The breaking point of each and every individual varies; John Doughty's tolerance had been tested to its extremity.

7

THE CAROLINE CARVER MYSTERY

DEATH BY DROWNING AT WAPPENSTALL, AUGUST 1935

Drowning is a common cause of death, generally accidental or suicide but, far more rarely, murder. Rare because a certain degree of physical strength is required to drown a healthy adult, unless the victim is first knocked unconscious, but little effort is required to push a frail or drunken person from a boat, or even, as we shall see, from a river bank.

Drowning is an unpleasant death. It is caused by the ingestion of water which mixes with the existing contents of the air passages, creating a liquid which causes convulsions and choking. Starved of oxygen the victim lapses into unconsciousness, quickly followed by death. Drowning is hastened by the struggles of the victim, who in panic tries to take in great gulps of air, but only succeeds in swallowing water.

The corpse will at first sink from the effects of water-filled lungs, remaining under the water for a short time before again floating to the surface as gases within the body expand, and the corpse takes on a bloated appearance. It is during this period that bodies are usually discovered. After remaining afloat for a while the body again sinks under water. In an attempt to prevent discovery a murderer may first knock his victim unconscious, then weight the body down before throwing it into the water.

One can well imagine the problems investigating police officers and forensic scientists face at the scene of a drowning incident. For example, little if any evidence will be available at the alleged crime scene, unless of course the body is discovered close to a river bank or similar location, where there may be direct evidence of a struggle. Unfortunately, most of the evidence is upon the human remains fished from the water. Minute examination of the body may lead to a suspect or conclusion as to the cause of death. It is also possible for a victim to drown in just a few inches of water, provided that the air passages are submerged, but such cases are rare.

Post-mortems can confirm or deny the alleged cause of death. Clearly, if a victim has been murdered elsewhere, then dumped in the water, no water will have been taken into the lungs, as no breathing would have taken place. The worst situation possible for all investigators is the decomposition of the corpse which putrefies fairly quickly in water, thus destroying so much evidence as to affect seriously the success of a post-mortem examination. Such are the problems facing many crime investigations; individual circumstances dictate that nothing is taken at face value, nothing can be presumed.

The scientific resources we have available today were not always so readily available to those involved in the investigating of crime and of murder in days gone by.

Edgmond is a small village situated three miles west of the town of Newport, which itself is located on the mid-eastern boundary of Shropshire, Edgmond being something of a dormitory village for Newport. Both are splendidly picturesque and ideal for a leisurely stroll, especially during a pleasant autumn or summer evening. Like so many similar villages, its quaint cottages and environment are not easily associated with murder, yet in 1935 such a charge was brought against a local man. A case which to this day still arouses some debate among those who discuss it.

Charles Carver, a local shepherd, resided at Stone House, 13 Marsh Road, Edgmond. He had lived there for several years along with his brother Richard. The pair were decent enough chaps, causing few if any problems within the local community. Charlie Carver gained some mild notoriety by his habit of tramping around the countryside at odd times of day and night, very often a little worse for wear, having over-indulged in his favourite refreshment, alcohol. This is the reason for his notoriety, as all too often it seemed that he had not the faintest idea where he was or what he was doing. Despite this, he seemed to be a harmless enough character who kept himself very much to himself when sober!

Richard Carver was not too dissimilar to his brother, though he was the quieter of the pair. In March 1934 the Carver brothers were forced to employ a housekeeper. Their parents being dead the two men found the chores of housekeeping as well as living a male orientated life style, too much of a burden. In 1934, a man was a man, it was he who provided for his family. The Victorian belief that a woman's place was in the home was paramount in the Carver residence. Thus the brothers brought in a Birmingham-born woman as a live-in housekeeper.

The situation at Stone House drastically altered, as the 61 year old Charlie Carver found himself entering into a relationship with the 57 year old housekeeper. If we are to accept this for what it seems, the relationship was very much a whirlwind romance, for within the space of four weeks the couple had married, and were living together at the house.

Some believe that Caroline Carver was out to profit financially from the marriage. As next of kin she would on Charlie's death inherit his worldly possessions, which were not enormous, but rumoured to be sufficient to warrant him to be comfortable. Caroline Carver was no paragon of virtue, she had children from previous relationships, and was fond of taking a drink, hence she was hardly the naive kind, but more of a worldly-wise woman who knew what she was doing.

There were those who believed that Charlie was simply besotted by Caroline, the ultimate goal of sexual satisfaction distorting the reality of a situation which would tie him to this woman for the remaining years of his life.

Now, Charlie Carver, as we are already aware, kept himself very much to himself, and tried not to get other people involved in his personal business, hence to all intents and purposes, the average outsider would have believed that his relationship with Caroline was perfectly happy, yet behind the scenes all was not well. Charlie's liking for alcohol, and his wife's occasional indulgence ensured that the pair were regularly seen in and around the local inns and hostelries, all too often the worse for drink.

The couple had a regular routine, whereupon each Saturday afternoon or early evening they would go to nearby Newport for their shopping, this invariably meant visits to several public houses and more drink. On Saturday the 24th August 1935 the couple, as was normal, left their Marsh Road home in the afternoon, en route for Newport for the gathering of the weekly provisions. They were seen together in the Vine Vaults and the Swan Inn, both were consuming enough alcohol to convince onlookers that they were well on the way to being drunk. At around 8.15 pm on the same evening a local fisherman by the name of Trumper was sitting on the bank of the Shropshire Union Canal and later claimed to have seen Charlie and Caroline Carver walking along the towpath in the direction of the Edgmond Bridge. The pair were clearly agitated and were arguing. Trumper acted as though he was unaware of their presence and

The lonely road into Edgmond – the route walked by Charlie Carver after the last meeting with his wife.

attempted to concentrate on his evening's fishing. He may well have been the last person, other than Charlie Carver, to see Caroline alive, hence his evidence was of vital importance.

At 9 pm that same evening Charlie Carver was in the Bridge Inn, Newport where he had a quick drink and stayed for about ten minutes. Nobody there recalls him acting any differently than he normally did. He was in an inebriated state, but not to the extent where one could say drunk. Carver left the Bridge Inn and was next seen by neighbours in Marsh Road a short time later, explaining that he had 'lost his missus'!

News of Charlie's loss spread with some urgency; a search of the local pubs proved negative, and she was not with any of her female acquaintances. Typically, the neighbours were not too surprised by her disappearance for, as previously stated, she too liked a drink, and it was an obvious thought among those aware of her absence that she might be laid drunk somewhere. To put matters bluntly, nobody really cared, she was an adult and could look after herself.

Charlie Carver decided that it was in his best interests to report his wife's disappearance to the police, and spoke to Police Sergeant Taylor and Constable Addison, explaining his predicament. The officers remained cool, calm and collected, took down a good description of the missing woman and duly disseminated this, though with little urgency, for many people fail to come home during a weekend's social activities.

Within a few hours matters took a dramatic turn as rumours spread throughout the community that a woman's body had been found in the Shropshire Union Canal on the Wappenstall side of the Edgmond Bridge. Two brothers had discovered the body lying in shallow water. It was immediately recognisable as being that of Caroline Carver. The police were called to the scene, and in time-honoured tradition, moved away a small crowd of curiosity seekers. The area was cordoned off as well as possible, and a doctor called to attend. Within the space of an hour the remains were positively identified as being those of Caroline Carver, and she was pronounced dead. The police carried out a thorough examination of the scene where the body was found. There were no obvious signs of a struggle on the canal bank, no slide marks in the mud, no flattened grass, no lumps or divots removed by someone involved in a scuffle, clutching for something to maintain stability. Closer examination of the corpse revealed virtually damning evidence that this was not an accident; Caroline Carver had no mud on the soles of her shoes, thus negating the possibility that she had wandered into the water of her own accord, unless of course, she had launched herself off the canal bank and dived into the muddy, fairly shallow, water, which was extremely unlikely judging by the alcoholic state in which she had previously been seen,

After the body had been removed from the water, having sought guidance from senior officers, the police arrested Charlie Carver on suspicion of the murder of his wife Caroline. It was a devastating blow to the community, was it really possible that Charlie could kill his wife?

A post-mortem examination was carried out upon the remains of Caroline by Dr John Read Poole of Newport, whose official report contained little if anything conclusive; 'No sign of poison or anything similar, no obvious marks of violence. The mouth was empty, the tongue swollen, teeth clenched, brain normal, larynx choked with semi-digested food which extended into the windpipe. Water in lungs'. The classic symptoms associated with drowning were evident, yet nothing sinister to denote that she may have been deliberately thrown into the water, or held beneath the surface. The case against Charlie Carver was more than a little ambiguous, yet the police were of the opinion that he must have had some connection with the drowning.

At the subsequent trial, Charlie Carver told the crowded courtroom that the fisherman, Trumper, must have been mistaken, as he was most certainly not the person Trumper had seen with Caroline. He further claimed that he had been nowhere near the towpath that particular night, but had left Caroline at the Newport Bridge, from where he visited the Bridge Inn until shortly after 9 pm. He had then gone to the Kings Head before returning home. He told how Caroline had just returned from a stay with her daughter in Birmingham and that she had been curiously quiet and moody since coming back to Edgmond a few days prior to her death. He believed that she had something on her mind, but she had refused to tell him what it was. Amazingly, Carver then stated that Caroline had been drinking heavily on the night in question and that it was his personal opinion that she had fallen into the water!

Several character witnesses were presented by the defence, all stated that they did not think it possible for Charlie Carver to commit murder and that apart from his drinking he was, in their opinion, a reasonably honest and loyal individual.

The prosecution were hard pushed to produce evidence which would clearly indicate Carver's guilt. The fisherman Trumper found his evidence analysed and then seemingly ignored as Carver had claimed that he was mistaken.

As a result of this, and Carver's excellent self representation when in the witness stand, the jury found him not guilty, and he duly walked out of the Shrewsbury Court a free man.

We shall never truly know just what happened that autumn evening by the Shropshire Union Canal. Did Charlie Carver find his lustful desire for Caroline to be dwindling, and the marital strain placed upon their relationship by her having a family elsewhere too great for him to handle? It certainly seems that way, after all, someone was arguing with Caroline along the towpath that night. Charlie had, by his own admission, been with her most of the day and evening in question, and further admitted walking with her towards the area where her body was later found. Are we to believe that someone else, matching his description, met her and almost instantly began arguing with her? I think not. Charlie Carver was a fortunate man, he alone held the key to the mystery of his wife's death, accidental or not, he must have known more than he ever admitted. His reactions after the event were surely nothing more than a sham, a deliberate deceit. Perhaps this was a case of the 'perfect murder', if such a thing is humanly possible.

I am certain that with today's scientific knowledge brought to bear on the available evidence, a more damning conclusion would have been reached on the involvement of Charlie Carver in his wife's death.

8

DEADLY LOVE

THE MURDER OF DOROTHY CLEWES
AT MARKET DRAYTON, APRIL 1936

Obsessional love, especially when that love is not reciprocated, can be deadly. Frustrated in his or her affections, the obsessed one may turn to violence, determined that if they cannot have the desired object, no one else shall possess it.

Weapons may be resorted to, perhaps the most common of these being fire-arms. In this country the use of guns is strictly controlled, but most readily available is the shot-gun, widely used in agricultural areas for the destruction of pests and vermin. A shot-gun can be adapted as a murder weapon by sawing off the barrel, though if care is not taken the process can be extremely dangerous; if sawn too short there is the distinct possibility that the gun may kick back and explode in the user's face. In recent years the sawn-off shot-gun has been synonymous with violent crime, in particular with bank robberies and hold-ups.

Anyone suffering from the effects of a shot-gun wound, with its multiplicity of pellets, is to say the least in a great deal of physical distress, and as we shall see, unless prompt and skilled medical attention is available, the wounds can prove fatal.

Market Drayton is a thriving town with at least one building dating back to the 16th century, but it can be traced back as far as Saxon times. It received its market charter around 1245. However, it is not the archetypal old market town, as it also possesses a thoroughly modern shopping centre.

The Easter of 1936 was a fairly quiet one in Market Drayton with the main topic of conversation being the trial of Dr Buck Ruxton in Lancashire, a murderer who had killed his wife and servant before chopping them into tiny pieces and depositing them in a stream in Scotland. It was a horrific crime avidly reported in the pages of the

71

national press. The residents of the market town were to experience the horror of a murder committed in their own surroundings, a crime so unnecessary, and quite unbelievable.

Dorothy Clewes was a likeable young girl, aged just 18. She was popular among the youth of Market Drayton, and with a vivacious outgoing personality she had plenty of friends, added to which there were plenty of boys competing for her attention. But Dorothy was a cautious girl and selected her friends carefully.

For a short time, Dorothy had been courting a young man of her own age, a farm labourer named Ernest Robert Hill of Moreton Wood. The relationship had been finished by Dorothy on the Good Friday of 1936, after an argument in which Hill accused Dorothy of exchanging flirtatious glances with another youth. Hill was obsessed with his girlfriend to the extent that he became paranoid about her being unfaithful to him.

Dorothy found his obsession and insecurity too much to bear. She had not so much as glanced at anyone else and told Hill this. The farm labourer, now in a jealous frenzy, grabbed hold of her arm and squeezed it so tightly that Dorothy cried out in pain, and was bruised by the grip. This violent outburst was the final straw, and Hill was duly despatched, and expelled from Dorothy's thoughts.

To most people, that would be the matter forgotten, for Hill must have known he had overstepped the mark; unnecessary violence, be it towards a woman, child or member of the same sex, is foolhardy and displays a lack of self-control. The fact that Hill was but 18 years of age and somewhat immature may explain this particular outburst, but Ernest Robert Hill was no ordinary 18 year old; inside he was a simmering mixture of emotions – emotions which were about to boil over.

On the morning of Easter Monday 1936, Hill had seen Dorothy in Market Drayton. She had been wearing lipstick and was dressed as though going out on a date; friends had told him that Dorothy had another boyfriend! Hill was seething, but continued on his way.

Later in the afternoon of that same day, Dorothy was out walking with her sister Florrie and a good friend, Phyllis Garrett. The trio were walking abreast along the country road between Market Drayton and Tern Hill; everything was fine, it was a warm enough afternoon and the girls were enjoying the tranquillity. Suddenly Ernest Hill cycled up behind them and as he passed gave a cold stare directed at Dorothy. The group were about one and a half miles out

Tern Hill Road, Market Drayton – the scene today.

of Market Drayton, and in the middle of nowhere, albeit they were in the parish of Moreton Say.

Hill pedalled on for about 50 yards before stopping the cycle, dismounting, and leaning it against a fence by Birch Tree Stile. He then turned to face the approaching girls, and stood in a threatening manner, legs slightly apart and his right hand tucked inside his overcoat pocket. It was clear some form of confrontation was about to take place, but the girls continued to walk towards Tern Hill. As they neared the waiting youth, he crossed the road to stand in front of them as though creating a physical barrier preventing them from going any further. Calmly he approached Dorothy and said, 'Hello'.

Before the girls could realise what was happening, Hill produced a sawn-off shot-gun from within his right overcoat pocket. He pointed it directly towards Dorothy's left breast, so close that it was actually touching the material of her dress. Florrie Clewes told Hill to stop being so stupid and attempted to pull Dorothy away, when suddenly the peace of the countryside was destroyed by a sickening crack; Hill had squeezed the trigger and had shot Dorothy in the region of her left upper arm.

The wounded girl collapsed to the ground, while the other two girls screamed in horror. Suddenly this peaceful road had turned into a scene of bloodshed. Crows and other birds, startled by the gunshot squawked and screamed as they circled the area in terror, while in a natural act of self-preservation, Ernest Hill replaced the gun in his coat pocket, crossed the road, climbed back upon his cycle and rode off without uttering a single word.

Dorothy's dress had caught fire from the effect of the shot-gun

SALOP BOY SENTENCED TO DEATH

—

ERNEST ROBERT HILL, 18-years-old farm labourer, was sentenced to death at Salop Assizes this afternoon for the murder at Moreton Say on April 13th of Dorothy Clewes, aged 18, his former sweetheart.

The jury added a strong recommendation to mercy, and the question of an appeal is being considered.

Hill shot the girl with a sawn-off shot-gun, and she died in hospital from tetanus.

His mother collapsed when she heard the verdict, and a woman juror was also affected.

[Full story on page 7.]

Contemporary newspaper coverage of the final day of the trial.

being fired so close to her arm. This was quickly extinguished, but she was in great distress and quickly lapsed into shock as the blackened and crimson coloured hole in her arm glistened in the sunlight.

Within minutes assistance had been summoned and Dorothy was on her way to Market Drayton cottage hospital to receive the medical attention she so desperately required. A handkerchief was placed over the gaping wound in her arm to prevent further loss of blood and to prevent bacteria from entering it – whether this was the correct course of action is questionable for doubts must be raised (and were) as to the cleanliness of the handkerchief.

The hospital removed some 99 pellets from her arm, and apart from shock, Dorothy's condition was fairly stable, although still serious. News of the shooting reached the police, statements were recorded and Constable Jones duly visited Ernest Hill at his home, where the constable searched Hill's overcoat and found the offending weapon and arrested him. Hill openly admitted the attack and was held in custody pending further enquiries and a court appearance.

On Tuesday the 21st of April, Dorothy's condition suddenly deteriorated, and she died two days later. Hill was then charged with the unlawful killing of Dorothy Clewes, a crime then punishable by death.

A post-mortem was carried out by Dr Edgar Conningsby Myott of Stoke-on-Trent. He noted that there was burning at the entrance of the wound, and he duly took cultures from the injured limb for further testing. The lungs had haemorrhaged beneath the pleura and on the pericardium. The vessels covering the brain were engorged and the glands in the mesentry were calcified. A short time later, as a result of the cultures removed from the wound, Dr Myott confirmed that he had found the presence of the bacillus of tetanus, and duly pronounced that death was a result of tetanus caused by the wound.

Ernest Hill continued to confess to his guilt, and said that he committed the crime because he did not like to see Dorothy wearing lipstick and make-up! He was subsequently tried and found guilty of murder with the maximum punishment by law being pronounced. It was revealed at the trial by Hill's defence that it was their belief the hospital had not maintained high medical standards, and that they had failed to treat the wound with doses of serum which could have prevented further infection setting in. There was also a discussion as to the condition of the handkerchief placed over the wound by persons at the scene.

The death of Dorothy Clewes was one of those crimes which are difficult to comprehend, clearly Ernest Hill was totally obsessed by the girl: he could not bear the thoughts of her seeing another man and dressing up to make herself attractive. A tragic end to a promising life. The wounds were not only limited to Dorothy, there were those invisible scars which her family would carry around for the rest of their lives.

9

TRAUMATIC TOOTHACHE!

THE DEATHS OF EDWARD AND THOMAS PERKINS AT MINSTERLEY, MARCH 1940

Toothache is one of the worst everyday pains the human body can suffer. It is of course a warning that all is not well with the mouth. Neuralgia is a separate problem which has a number of causes, though decayed teeth are generally to blame. A temporary remedy is to cover the gum area with oil of cloves, but the best treatment, if the offending tooth cannot be filled, is immediate extraction; the idea of which sends shivers up one's spine. The fear of dentists is common in our society, for the teeth are so sensitive that it is disagreeable to suffer anyone else to touch them, let alone drilling or grinding them. But agonising though it is, rarely does toothache lead to murder.

The village of Minsterley sits some eight miles to the south west of Shrewsbury on the A488. It is an old and pleasant village with some fine examples of 17th century architecture, particularly the hall and the church, both of which were built by the Thynne family. Minsterley has a mining background, with mineral extraction being one of the main industries in the region.

In 1940, the village was a fairly nondescript sort of place, with everyone knowing their neighbours, and there was no obvious disharmony within the daily life of the village. Thomas and Edward Perkins, who were aged 30 and 18 years respectively, lived together in The Hostel in the village. Their parents were both dead and a further brother, Jack, had moved away from the area some time earlier and now resided in Devon.

Thomas and Edward were reasonable enough young men, they enjoyed a drink, but had been raised with good old-fashioned family values, and both were best described as 'responsible'.

Minsterley today – more than fifty years after the terrible events of that March day, the village looks much the same.

Like most of the men in Minsterley and the surrounding area, the Perkins brothers worked in the baryte mine. Although they had no mother or wife to attend to their welfare the brothers had a friend, Mrs Richards who prepared their meals on a fairly regular basis, and they also employed a female cleaner.

The village of Minsterley woke to disaster on the morning of Good Friday 1940. Emma Betton was walking through the village and happened to glance towards the Perkins' residence when she saw a door open. Her suspicions were increased when she also noted that the curtains were drawn in every room of the house. This was contrary to the Perkins' routine; both men were early risers, and should by then have left the house, so the open door seemed rather suspicious.

Emma Betton continued on her way along the sunken road towards The Bog, a disused mine, when ahead of her she saw the bodies of two men slumped on the ground. Frantically she fled back towards Minsterley and ran up to The Hostel and cried out for help.

Receiving no response she ran on to the Miners Arms where she raised the alarm with landlord Mr Johnson who at once called for the police.

Within a few minutes a murder investigation unit was at the scene. The bodies, certified dead, were identified as those of Thomas and Edward Perkins; both had gunshot wounds in their foreheads. Edward Perkins' wound was such that it was clear he had committed suicide, the wound had scorch marks on the surrounding skin, causing a black discolouration. This only occurs when the barrel of the weapon is held close to or directly upon the flesh, the deposits charring the skin as the shot is fired. More conclusively, Edward Perkins still held the gun in his hand.

Examination of the bodies and of the wounds showed that it was impossible for Thomas to have shot himself; the injuries he had sustained confirmed that the weapon had been held at least three feet from his head, an impossible feat for him to have achieved.

Enquiries revealed that neither man had any serious enemies, and a search of their home revealed that everything was in its place, so far as could be ascertained there were no items of value absent, thus ruling out burglary or other criminal activity. The cleaner who regularly visited the house confirmed that nothing was amiss in The Hostel.

A cousin came forward and told how he had been drinking with the two men just two days before the incident, neither man showed any sign of being disturbed or concerned about anything, although Edward had complained of suffering the effects of a raging toothache. Indeed, further witnesses came forward with similar information; some told how Edward's face had appeared swollen, one man even stated that Edward appeared to be apathetic and to be lacking enthusiasm for life in general. He complained that his teeth were causing him so much pain as to affect his jaw and neck. Despite every effort, the police and other investigating authorities could find no criminal reason for the incident. Yes, they were aware that both men carried out a little nocturnal poaching activity in the surrounding countryside, but so did a lot of other people, and nobody would feel so upset about this as to commit murder!

No stone was left unturned, and a great deal of information came forward about the brothers, none of which was relevant to the enquiries. Residents of Shrewsbury were spoken to, also many publicans in whose hostelries the brothers would occasionally drink, yet not one solitary individual came forward with any motive for murder, quite simply, no motive seemed to exist. Thomas and

Edward Perkins were both highly thought of young men, albeit perhaps the memory and tragedy of losing both their parents tended to afford them a little more sympathy than was necessary.

The only conclusion the authorities could arrive at, was that Edward Perkins, incensed and ravaged by pain, had in a moment of excruciating anguish shot dead his elder brother, before realising what he had done, and then in remorse had punished himself by turning the gun on his own head.

It was and still remains a curious act, but quite simply there is no other solution possible, unless of course, someone somewhere has committed the perfect murder? Yet there is no such thing, and there were no strangers seen in the village at the approximate time of the incident. The killer in this case, was a tooth, decayed and rotten its agonising pain drove a generally sane man to destruction.

This course of action is not recommended as a relief for toothache.

10

THE PIN-STRIPE JACKET MYSTERY

THE MURDER OF BETTY SMITH AT ATCHAM, SEPTEMBER 1953

Strangulation, or throttling, is an uncommon form of murder, because of the physical strength required and the ability to overcome the struggles of the victim. To ensure success the victim's respiration must be cut off by crushing the carotid nerve plexuses, thus obstructing the blood flow to the brain. With a full-grown strong adult this is a near-impossible task, hence its unpopularity with would-be murderers. With a young child it is a more simple matter.

After such a murder, the killer is often preoccupied with covering his traces, he may set fire to the corpse, drop it in a lake or river, or bury it in the hope it may decompose, thus destroying evidence. The corpse of a strangulation victim can provide a great deal of evidence for the investigating authorities. Bruising to the neck and interior muscles indicates from what angle the murderer strangled his victim – the thumb and fingers leave marks where pressure has been applied to the neck, thus assisting the deduction process. But every murder is unique, and the police and forensic teams have to be alert for the less obvious.

Leaving Shrewsbury along the A5 and travelling in a south-easterly direction one soon arrives in the village of Atcham, where a 16th century seven-arched bridge is a sight to behold, not only from a historical but also a technological point of view, as one can only marvel at the ingenuity of the mind of the late John Gwynne who created it. The village image is further enhanced by the smooth running waters of the river Severn which passes through its boundaries. Atcham has to be one of the nicest places in Shropshire, its people are friendly, its buildings quaint, its streets clean and tidy; altogether a pleasant environment. One can imagine it has always

The river Severn near Atcham.

been so, although just 41 years ago such a wicked deed occurred here that should have left a black cloud of depression permanently hovering above the village.

Desmond Donald Hooper had always appeared to be a reasonable sort of chap. Aged 27 he was, or so it seemed, happily married with children and he resided in an army camp at Atcham. Hooper worked at the Copthorne barracks where a wartime military hospital was situated, and indeed still is, albeit overshadowed by the new Royal Shrewsbury Hospital which now dominates the skyline.

Desmond Hooper was an extremely keen pigeon fancier and he would spend long periods alone with his pigeons which could be seen circling the area for hours. The pigeons actually all belonged to a local man, a farmer called Harris who owned Attingham Home Farm. Hooper was welcome to assist with the pigeons and did so with great enthusiasm, and much of his spare time was spent at the farm. Pigeons are most interesting birds, which provide a satisfying hobby. Flying pigeons can initially prove frustrating, however with confidence and practice greater objectives are possible. At the start, the birds are usually taken a short distance from home and released just before their feed is due, hunger guiding them to their homes. Eventually the distance to be flown is increased. The pigeons are easily transported, even in a suitable basket on the carrier of a bicycle!

The Hooper family were on friendly terms with most other people in the camp but there was a particular partiality for a twelve year old girl called Elizabeth (Betty) Selina Smith, who would call round to their home and play with the children. Betty was a nice young girl, typically naive, but also very sensible in her manner and perceptions. Her parents never objected to her being at the Hoopers, for at the very least they knew she was safe and well.

It was around September 1953 that tragedy struck in Atcham. Accidents will happen no matter what precautions one takes. Only very misguided parents are over-protective and refuse to allow their children freedom, for young people are naturally inquisitive and tend to free themselves from restrictive family reins at the first opportunity. Obviously, parents wish to protect their children, but usually are wise enough to allow them some freedom of movement, as Mr and Mrs Smith did. People in the 1950s were not so aware of the sexual deviant and the psychopathic murderer as we are in today's society. Having said that, such individuals are rare and we should not entertain the belief that one lurks around each and every corner – they don't!

The first alarm bells began sounding in Atcham when Mrs Smith called round at the Hoopers' home one evening in search of her daughter, who she believed had called there for some magazines a short time earlier. Mrs Hooper knew nothing of it, she had been out, but Desmond had been in, perhaps he would know. Unfortunately it appeared that Desmond had gone out to tend the pigeons, some of which had not returned to the loft. He had left his wife a short note explaining that he was out searching for the missing birds.

Within a short while he returned and was greeted by Mrs Smith and his wife and was asked if he had seen anything of Betty. Hooper explained that she had in fact called round a little earlier but he had sent her home with some magazines as he had to leave the house in search of his beloved pigeons; this must have been about one and a half hours earlier, as he had walked to Attingham Home Farm, where he found the lost birds in the rafters of a barn but had been unable to retrieve them. Desmond Hooper was visibly shocked by Betty's disappearance and agreed to help look for the girl, all night if necessary.

Mrs Hooper also offered to help search the local area, and advised Mrs Smith to notify the police immediately, as for some reason, and one cannot condemn the unfortunate woman, she had delayed reporting her daughter missing, perhaps in the vain hope that she would be found without making anything official and thus arousing a great deal of unwanted attention.

Desmond Hooper took off into the cool night in search of the child he knew so well. But his frantic concern was a hypocritical farce played out in an attempt to cover a terrible secret he held deep within the confines of his sadistically sick mind. Desmond Hooper knew only too well where Betty Smith was: he had killed her, and honestly believed that he would never be found out!

The following day the police recorded an official missing persons (misper) report from the Smith family, and at once commenced a local search with a view to expanding as enquiries continued. A sympathetic officer recorded the various details and at once set about his enquiries. Starting with the last person to see Betty alive – Desmond Hooper.

Hooper told precisely the same story to the officer as he had told to his wife and Betty's mother: about his search for the lost pigeons, and how he had sent Betty home. House to house enquiries were carried out in the neighbourhood, and as time progressed the situation appeared to deteriorate, with no new information coming forward. At this stage it was nothing more than a missing persons enquiry. Abduction or any other crime were not yet suspected. It was at the back of everyone's mind that she may well have wandered off and had an accident and be lying somewhere injured or even dead!

The search area was expanded and within two days of her disappearance, the body of Betty Smith was found. The discovery was alerted by the locating of an adult's blue pinstripe jacket which lay at the top of an air shaft leading down into the Shropshire Union Canal. The body of the twelve year old girl was found within the cold waters of the Canal beneath the shaft, the body when removed clearly indicating that she had suffered some form of strangulation. A doctor was called to the scene and certified death. Meanwhile, an unfortunate police officer was faced with breaking the news to the Smith family, a ghastly task at the best of times, but made all the worse by the fact that Betty had been murdered!

The Smiths were asked to confirm that the body was that of their young daughter and duly did so. The word grief does not begin to express the emotional distress this poor family had to endure. Initially tortured by the disappearance of their own flesh and blood, and now destroyed by her senseless death at the hands of a sick killer, who, needless to say, nobody believed would be a local person.

A murder team was assembled and immediate house to house enquiries again commenced, this time, the questions would be a great deal more searching, and the answers assessed time and again, checked and double checked. Nobody was absolved of suspicion until they could conclusively prove their innocence, which may sound a little dramatic, but is necessary if investigators are to make any headway with their enquiries.

News of the murder spread far and wide, and was reported by the local and national press, with the police requesting anyone with information, no matter how obscure it might seem, to come forward and report it to them.

Desmond Hooper, having admitted to seeing and speaking with the murdered child, was the last person apart from her killer, to have seen her alive, so was the first person outside the Smith family to be spoken to. The family, unfortunately, always have to be questioned about a number of matters. Police officers, having experience of the remorse, guilt and grief which is present within families at such times, were astute enough to recognise that the Smith family was a good one, loving and caring, with nothing to hide. It was ascertained that Betty had no obvious enemies, neither had the family. Mrs Smith had expected Betty to return home fairly quickly from the Hoopers; no strangers had been seen in the area, and they suspected no one of their daughter's murder.

Desmond Hooper was visited; once again he maintained his story, but his grief seemed overly exaggerated, and he was too precise with his answers. Yet the police, at this stage, had nothing to go on. It is almost certain that they did suspect Hooper, but proving such suspicions is a totally different matter.

The blue pin-stripe jacket was shown off and anyone knowing a person who owned or wore such a jacket was urged to come forward. Several did so, including a motorist who saw a man and child near the air shaft on the night of the murder, the child had been wearing the jacket, which was clearly meant for an adult. It was also stated that the child did not appear to be in any distress, but was quite happy with her companion.

Wrapped round Betty Smith's neck had been a tie, used to strangle her, but investigations into the ownership of this item were even less successful than discovering the owner of the jacket.

Information was received from various sources that Desmond Hooper owned or wore a blue pin-striped jacket similar to the one found close to the murder scene, but so too did many men, including police officers investigating the crime. The ownership of such a jacket was far too flimsy a fact to indicate anyone's guilt.

Putting together the information they had at their disposal the police realised that the finger of guilt and suspicion was pointed at one person, Desmond Hooper, and so enquiries were commenced into his story. Police officers were sent to re-enact his movements and to talk with anyone who may have seen or heard him.

Attingham Home Farm was visited and Mr Harris spoken to, he had not seen nor heard Hooper on the evening in question, furthermore, he found it difficult to believe that anyone could have been in one of his barns as his farm dogs, who were extremely noisy and vigilant, had not barked. This was unusual if not unique, as they generally barked and barked if anyone approached or entered the yard. Mrs Lewis was also a resident on the farm and her private room faced on to the yard and barn where Hooper claimed to have been; she too had failed to see or hear anyone, and she also commented that if anyone had been there, the dogs would have barked! At last, the police had found a chink in Hooper's alibi.

Desmond Hooper was arrested on suspicion of murder and later charged with the same offence. During the subsequent investigations, his seven year old son happened to mention that he had witnessed his father send Betty Smith home. This seemed a major development, but was quickly proved to be inaccurate as the boy explained that his father had told him to say this!

At his trial, Desmond Donald Hooper denied murder. Various attempts were made to prove his innocence, but the police had carried out a very thorough investigation, and clearly proved the case against the defendant. Evidence showed that he had physically strangled the child, using his tie as a type of garrotte, then depositing her body head first down the air shaft and into the cold waters of the canal. Found guilty he was sentenced to death; his appeal against the sentence failed, and he was executed at Shrewsbury in January 1954.

It was a disgusting and despicable crime, with deviant motives. To take the life of one so vibrant and young and with a sense and knowledge of life is unforgivable. Hooper met with the just reward for his sins, although as one resident of present day Atcham told me, 'Capital punishment in some cases is far too easy an option for such wicked individuals; the feeling in the community at the time, correct or not, was an eye for an eye, Hooper died too easily.'

The murder in Atcham is not only about Desmond Hooper, and his sick actions, but also about the tragic loss forced upon devoted parents. Sadly, today such losses still occur, but with what punishment?

11

DRUNK AND DISORDERLY

THE MURDER OF MRS SMITH AT COPTHORNE, OCTOBER 1960

Alcohol, unless one is very careful, can be addictive. Alcoholics become obsessed with its mind-numbing effect and can lose everything – destruction of a relationship, a career, or in some extreme cases, life itself!

It has the effects of a drug, causing emotions from elation to depression, anger to remorse, none of these a true picture of the person's character, which becomes submerged beneath the effects of intoxication. Problems are forgotten and the mundaneness of life disappears with each drink; the world can be a happier, more pleasing place – but for how long? Once the effects wear off the suffering starts. Reality slaps you in the face; nothing has changed except that money has been wasted, there is the excruciating despair of a hangover and often self-disgust. During a bout of drunkenness inhibitions are lost and violence may be resorted to.

When this occurs it can be extreme; reason having been lost in the poisonous fumes of alcohol. When attacking another person the assailant may rain blows on his victim and if directed on the same area these may have the effect of bludgeoning, causing serious tissue damage. Rarely do such blows kill, unless prolonged and aimed at a vulnerable area.

Shrewsbury has had an unfair association with killers throughout its history, perhaps because as a county town it has been the epicentre of social activities in the surrounding communities, or perhaps because it is just plain unlucky. Whatever the reason, compared to many of its contemporaries its streets and houses have seen some horrific crimes, none more so than one which occurred in autumn 1960 in the Copthorne district of the town.

Copthorne hospital today – once an army camp. George Riley knew this area well and often visited the base.

George Riley was a young man living at home with his family, he was still learning his trade as a butcher in the town and was a typically excitable youngster who thought of nothing else but enjoying himself. Young people often have a tendency to over-indulge in alcohol, as though they must prove just how much they can consume in front of their friends. Sensible folk are of course aware of the perils of such activity, but most young men go through this stage, indeed this author was such a typical young man!

Social gatherings, when one is so young, are of great importance; dances are places were men can meet women, drink, dance and generally enjoy themselves. Pubs are there to be visited during the week when no dances are available. Alternatively they are places to visit prior to a dance, a place to get merry. As one gets older, pubs and dances take on a totally different aspect (or they should) but still provide a source of entertainment.

One Friday night in October 1960, pay night, George Riley returned to his Westland Street home and handed over his 'keep' to his mother, and gave her some savings stamps which he had also purchased, to save for him. Riley was a fairly reasonable young man with some common sense, his parents had taught him the value of money and to save a little each week. Riley had accepted this advice and duly handed over a percentage of his wages each Friday. The remainder was there for him to fritter away on his social and leisure activities.

After eating his meal Riley got changed and was soon answering a knock at the front door, it was Tony Brown, a good friend of George's. Brown owned a car which was an attractive proposition for young men, as to their naive minds it impressed members of the opposite sex, it was a status object, almost a phallic symbol.

The two men were 'out on the town' and intended to 'pull' (to attract a female partner). As it was still early evening it seemed pointless to go to a dance at such an hour. They discussed which dance they should attend and both decided to visit the Sentinel works dance at Harlescott, but first they had the opportunity of having a few drinks.

The pair toured several pubs in Shrewsbury before making their way to the dance. It has to be said that George Riley was well on his way to being drunk by the time he visited the dance. He was in a boisterous frame of mind, and was making a good deal of noise, all good humoured banter, but annoying to some. More drinks were consumed in the dance, rendering Riley drunk, and if it was at all possible, more drunk than he had ever been. Tony Brown claimed that he took in somewhere in the region of nine pints of beer, eight whiskies, and some soft drinks. Enough to render any normal man totally incapacitated and unable to make any sound judgement.

George, by this stage, had sailed through the happy period of drunkenness and was fast approaching delirium, but not without first becoming antagonistic and squaring up for a fight. Another local man, Laurence Griffiths, took up Riley's challenge: he too was drunk and both men fell to the floor and acted out a farcical wrestling bout, with neither able to project any force or power into the limp blows they aimed at each other. Both were clearly angry, but incapable of doing anything about it.

Several more sober folk split the fight, which to the outsider may have had the appearance of women cuddling on the floor. Tony Brown moved George Riley away from his opponent and attempted to calm him down, but Riley was unheeding. His mind was set upon

George Riley.

fighting, false bravado, Dutch courage, call it what you will, he wanted to fight, to take on the world and beat it. He aroused the anger of several other men in the dance before being dragged outside. It is therefore curious to note that two policemen who were in attendance at the dance felt that Riley was reasonably sober and in control of his actions, and although drunk, he was not paralytic.

It was around 1.30 am when the men left the dance, Riley had stopped drinking and had perhaps begun to sober up, rather than sink deeper into oblivion. Tony Brown took home other friends from the dance and dropped George outside his home, bidding him goodnight. By this time Riley was able to stand and speak without staggering or slurring his words.

George Riley stood in the street, the cold night air having a sobering effect upon him, as he reached inside his trouser pocket, his fingers scrabbling about inside the lining for the jagged metal object that was his key.

Looking around his attention was drawn to a house opposite where a middle-aged widow, Mrs Smith, resided. George had often been into her home in search of change and for a general chat. God only knows what went through his mind, but the search for his key only showed him that he had just a few coins in his pocket; he had wasted much of his wages on one night's drinking, what was he to do for the rest of the week?

Riley knew that Mrs Smith kept a purse in her handbag in her bedroom, and for some unknown reason decided that he would enter her home and take this money while she slept. In other words he would become a common night-time burglar. Only desperate persons need to commit such avaricious and cowardly acts; those whose mentality and intelligence are questionable. Hence George Riley, full of drink and his mind completely befuddled.

Riley smashed a window pane of a rear facing french window to Mrs Smith's premises and quietly entered her bedroom, searching for the handbag, which he found difficult to locate in the dim glow from the street lights. Eventually he found it and was angry when he saw that the purse contained but a few shillings.

Without warning, Mrs Smith sat bolt upright in bed and saw George Riley delving into her bag. She flung herself at him in an attempt to detain him and cried out. The words had barely left her lips when she was struck a vicious blow to her face which caused her to recoil in shock and anguish. She maintained her hold on Riley, although by now more in an act of desperation than anything threatening. Riley struck her across the face again and again until she let go. Eventually the defenceless Mrs Smith collapsed on the floor semi-conscious, her face bleeding profusely. George Riley, angry, upset and frightened, vented his feelings upon the woman who lay at his feet. He knelt above her and punched her repeatedly until she made no more noise and her face was unrecognisable as being that of a living person. Blood splattered the walls and surrounding furniture, and in a final act of outrage, Riley tore at the woman's nightdress, exposing parts of her body. Several of her teeth had been knocked into her throat, others lay on the floor within the pool of dark red blood which poured from her bludgeoned head.

In a complete state of panic, Riley then left via the broken window and ran across the fields, without stopping until he reached the locality of a public house at Bicton. Eventually, now fully aware of his actions, he returned home, but once again failed to locate his door key, so slept in the garage of the family home, which offered more sanctuary than the cold October streets of Copthorne.

Early the next morning, he banged at a window of the house until his brother let him in. He then went to his bed, where, amazingly, he fell asleep without any conscience.

Olive Martin was the sister of Mrs Smith, the pair were fairly close and Miss Martin had spent part of the previous day with her sister, leaving her at around 7.30 pm. They had arranged to go out on the Saturday morning, so Olive Martin telephoned the house, but received no reply. She found this curious, as her sister was generally an early riser. Further calls remained unanswered, so she decided to go round and to waken her by knocking on the door. By now it was around 10 am. Olive Martin hammered on the door, but again received no reply. Seeing that the window curtains were all drawn, most unusual for her sister, Olive called upon a neighbour and asked if she had seen or heard from Mrs Smith that morning, the response was negative; nobody had seen her, and almost everyone commented upon how unusual it was for her not to be up and about by 10 am.

Olive Martin went to the police and soon returned with Sergeant Bean, who immediately looked for an obvious access point to the property. Accompanied by Olive Martin, he went to the rear of the house and found the smashed window in the french doors. Tentatively placing his hand through the jagged edges of the splintered glass, he opened the door and entered the house. Olive went upstairs and screamed in horror as she saw her sister's body upon the floor of her bedroom.

The house was at once sealed off, senior officers called to the scene, and a doctor pronounced life extinct. Fingerprint marks and other possible evidence were searched for, and house to house enquiries commenced. Not unnaturally the police were keen to speak with George Riley, having discovered that he had possibly been the last one up and about in the street that fateful morning. Riley was more than obstructive with his response to the enquiries, and as a matter of course the police asked him what he had been wearing that night. Reluctantly he produced first his shoes, which were covered in mud, his trousers, similarly plastered, and his jacket and shirt, which clearly bore blood stains. Riley could not account for these and was arrested on suspicion of murder.

Initially he denied all charges, but agreed to make a statement which he never signed. Realising that he was not to escape justice he told the truth but proffered the excuse that he was not in proper control of his faculties through being drunk; ordinarily he would be on friendly terms with the widow Smith and was not a violent person. But this murder was not the ordinary action of any normal human being, but of a sadistic killer who continually beat his victim until she could take no more! A ring on his finger had exacerbated the wound, tearing into the flesh and gouging great lumps out. It was a sad end for such a kind and honest woman, who in all probability would have given Riley the money without hesitation, had he bothered to ask!

At his subsequent trial, which took place at Stafford as it was deemed a trial in Shropshire would be detrimental to his case because of the intense feeling against him there, George Riley offered his drunkenness as a defence, and received some sympathy, but the simple fact was that he was a murderer, a crime for which there was then but one sentence. Found guilty, he appealed, but this was refused and he was executed at Shrewsbury.

Mitigating circumstances? Justifiable excuse? I think not. Riley received the correct judgement and sentence for his abhorrent actions.

12

MURDER AT RHOS COTTAGE

**THE MURDERS OF JENNIFER VENABLES AND WILLIAM BUFTON
AT CHURCHBANK, JUNE 1939**

Clun is tucked away in the south-western district of Shropshire, a place of great historical interest which can claim to have a river and a forest named after it. It is a quaint town, filled with old and modern buildings, and it is a busy place, that is to say that everyone appears committed to their individual and respective tasks. Market day is on Tuesday,when a wide range of goods can be bought, Clun market is one of the nicest I have ever visited; stall holders prepared to stop and chat and showing a real interest in your requirements.

In June 1939 the peace and tranquillity of this charming little town were destroyed by the astonishing news that there had been a double murder in the Churchbank area. Gossip and rumour were rife as the tale of the discovery of the bodies altered with each new relation. First of all it was a burglary, then it was a fire, then an accident, then, in all probability, it was the lot. The truth of the matter did not emerge for several hours, and even then it was somewhat confusing.

A local butcher, Charles Wells had a roundsman carrying out his daily deliveries to the surrounding district. Wells' butchers was a good traditional type of village shop, indeed they were perhaps one of the finest purveyors of meats in the county, and their meat was ordered for miles around. The roundsman William (Billy) Bufton was another friendly chap, his round was a varied one and took him to several out of the way locations. However, this burden was eased by his ability to call for the odd cup of tea and a chat with various customers, one of whom was Mrs Jennifer Venables of Rhos Cottage, Pen-y-Wern, in Churchbank; Bufton often spoke warmly of the woman. Mr Venables also enjoyed Bufton's visits to the cottage for there was nothing suspicious about Bufton's friendship with his wife.

95

The butcher's shop at Clun, where Billy Bufton worked.

Mr Venables was a farm labourer and would cycle over twelve miles to his work and back. A dedicated and fit man, he was loyal to his employers, family and friends, and he expected loyalty in return; indeed he was extremely well respected by all who knew him.

Thus the situation was quite a happy one. Clun and the surrounding districts were happy places; no animosity, just friendly good-natured folk leading their own lives, typical of many places in the United Kingdom.

Charlie Wells noted that Billy Bufton was late returning from his round, to such a degree that Wells began to grow concerned for him. Not that he could have come to any harm but more the fact that he may have been involved in a breakdown and be stranded. So Wells, along with his father and son, jumped in their van and drove off in search of Billy. Having looked in all the usual places, he elected to try Churchbank in case he had decided to visit Mr and Mrs Venables.

Sure enough, the butcher's van was sat outside the cottage. Charlie

Wells knocked on the front door of the cottage but could raise no response from inside. He called out, but again received no reply. He then peered through the small windows and into the cottage living quarters, but could see no sign of movement. By now, uneasiness was growing inside him, and so he moved around the cottage and peered through another window. It took a moment for him to realise what he was looking at, for there in the kitchen lay the body of Jennifer Venables. Within a few seconds with adrenalin pumping through him at a furious rate, he forced open the front door to the cottage and entered the kitchen area.

It is possibly just as well that Charlie Wells was a butcher and used to seeing blood and gore, for there beneath the kitchen table lay the dead bodies of Jennifer Venables and Billy Bufton. Bufton lay with half of his head missing, presumably blown off by a shotgun. Mrs Venables' injuries were equally as horrific; she had a major wound in her chest, exposing much of her respiratory organs. The kitchen resembled a slaughter house, and Wells could not understand why or who could have done such a thing.

The police were notified and a doctor called to pronounce life extinct; neither victim could have suffered, as death must have been instantaneous. The police too, were at a loss as to the motive for the crime, nothing had been unlawfully removed from either the cottage or the bodies of the victims, and Bufton's van was still intact and complete with contents.

An inquest was held at Bishop's Castle and Wells gave his version of events as he knew them. No gun was located at the scene, and despite a thorough police search, it had not yet surfaced. This made it a clear case of murder, as with two dead bodies in the cottage, both suffering from gunshot wounds, but with no gun at the scene, someone had to have removed it, presumably the killer.

During the police investigation, it became clear that Bufton had one enemy within the community, a man known as George Owen, a county council employee who worked on the roads, and was a relation by marriage of the murdered man. Owen was currently in hospital at Shrewsbury, having attempted to take his own life by cutting his throat. He had in recent times become a thoroughly miserable man, perhaps through the strain of looking after an invalid wife and raising a family. The attempted suicide had been overlooked in the confusion of the murders at Churchbank, but was of no surprise to those who knew him, for he had become depressed with his lot and had often talked of doing away with himself.

As they occurred within hours of each other, the police linked the

Alleged Double Murder In Salop Cottage

TWO MEN ON "FRIENDLY TERMS" WITH WOMAN
—Prosecution

GEORGE OWEN, a middle-aged roadman, of 9, Woodside, Clun, was charged at Clun Police Court today with the murder of Mrs. Martha Jane Venables (52), of Rhos Cottage, Black Hill, and of William Frank Gerrard Bufton (32), a butcher's roundsman, of Castle-street, Clun.

Owen was also charged with attempted suicide.

Only a few members of the general public were admitted to the little court room. Twenty-six witnesses are being called, and the proceedings are expected to last until well into tomorrow.

Mr. Parham appeared for the Director of Public Prosecutions, and Mr. J. F. Bourke defended.

The Earl of Powis was a member of the bench of seven magistrates.

In his opening statement Mr. Parham said that Owen and Bufton were connected by marriage, Owen being an uncle of Bufton's wife.

On Tuesday, June 27th, Mr. Charles Wells, the butcher by whom Bufton was employed, went to Rhos Cottage and discovered the bodies.

The woman had been shot in the abdomen and the man had part of his face blown away. Both had been dead for some time.

TWO SHOTS HEARD

At 1.55 p.m. on June 27th Bufton called at a cottage in the neighbourhood of Rhos Cottage and was later seen going to Mrs. Venables' home.

At 2.15 two shots were heard. Owen, said Mr. Parham, was employed on roads in the neighbourhood of the cottage, and at one o'clock or soon after that day he was near the cottage because fresh cut gorse was found.

Owen was on friendly terms with Mrs. Venables, and when working near the cottage he used to have his meals there and also store his tools.

Bufton also was on friendly terms with Mrs. Venables, and there was no doubt, continued Mr. Parham, that the accused felt ill-will towards him, because he had been heard to utter threats and on one occasion he was heard to say he was going to shoot Bufton.

Mr. Parham said that while the police were at Venables's cottage they were called to Owen's home, and found Owen suffering from a cut in his throat. They would hear from a doctor that the wound was self-inflicted, though Owen said that the butcher's boy did it in the afternoon.

A shotgun, which had been recently fired, was found in the house, and two spent cartridges were discovered between the house and Rhos Cottage.

Expert evidence would be given that they were fired from the gun found in Owen's home.

Concluding, Mr. Parham said that when Owen was taken to the infirmary three handkerchiefs — belonging to a woman— were found among his clothing. One was identical with a handkerchief which it was known Mrs. Venables possessed.

NEAR THE COTTAGE

Evidence was given by Derek Horton George, an insurance agent, who said that at 1.10 p.m. on Tuesday, June 27th, he saw Owen working about 100 yards from Mrs. Venables' cottage.

(Proceeding).

The local press report of the opening day of the trial.

two incidents and a search of the grounds of Owen's cottage revealed a broken shotgun and cartridges. The police waited for Owen to leave hospital, his self-inflicted injury had been a cry for help, and was neither serious nor life-threatening.

When spoken to, Owen initially denied the crime, he claimed that he had borrowed the gun from a friend to kill rabbits. The rumours of Owen's dislike for Bufton were checked out, and several people told how Owen had verbally threatened to one day kill the butcher's roundsman, claiming him to be idle and a parasite, wasting time at Rhos Cottage when he should be out delivering meat or doing something more useful. It was a pathetic threat, and not one which anyone could seriously believe would be fulfilled.

Owen was arrested and charged with the double murder. Rhos Cottage was located on the piece of road which Owen covered for the local council; he had the ideal opportunity to commit the crime.

Owen, by this stage, was a demented lunatic; his mind had finally snapped. Perhaps when he pulled the trigger of the shotgun on that fateful afternoon and had witnessed the bloody scene he had created it was just too much for his mind to take.

He was brought before the Shropshire Assizes in November 1939, but was deemed unfit to plead. He was the killer, of that there was no doubt; he had confessed as much to the authorities. Mr Justice Lawrence instructed that he should be imprisoned during His Majesty's Pleasure.

13

THE BLACK PANTHER

THE KIDNAP AND MURDER OF LESLEY WHITTLE
AT DUDLEY, JANUARY 1975

The leopard is one of the most adaptable predators in the world, varying its diet according to the environment, and occasionally scavenging from the outskirts of towns and villages. Such is its cunning and strength that it can drag its prey up into the boughs of trees, away from its rivals. One form of leopard is melanistic – the black panther.

Asphyxiation as a cause of death can happen in a number of ways, perhaps the most common is by hanging. Many such deaths are suicides or accidental, through foolish pranks or sexual fantasies. This may seem a bizarre, almost unbelievable observation, however a small but significant number of people do have sado-masochistic tendencies, in particular the enjoyment to be obtained from pressure being placed on the carotid arteries, restricting blood flow and taking the participant to the brink of unconsciousness. The sexual deviancies of individuals practised in private are of no concern to the general public, who would be surprised at the number of people who practise this form of self-abuse, using ligatures to take themselves to the limits of agony, and ecstasy, before releasing the pressure and regaining their senses – though on occasion this is left too late and death intervenes.

Hanging is a reasonably uncommon method of murder because of the degree of physical work the killer has to undertake. Such a complex murder demands physical confrontation, manipulation and cunning, so is an understandably unpopular method. The crime scene at such an incident is usually straightforward as so much evidence is and can be made available to investigators by the fact that

Beech Croft, Highley – the Whittle family home.

hanging requires a great deal of preparation, thus leaving traces for forensic examination.

There is always the exception to the rule, where a killer is so devious, calculating and downright evil as to successfully cover his tracks. Though thankfully few in number, when such individuals do surface they pose a real threat to society. Intelligent police research into the psychology of these people has greatly assisted in understanding the hows and the whys of their behaviour; how they may react, where they may live, and what drives them to kill. Such analysis may even identify what background they may hail from.

There are not too many people who can be described as truly evil, cold and calculating killers, the individual we are about to discuss is one of England's worst. Driven by a lust for wealth and power, he destroyed several lives.

Highley is not one of the most aesthetically pleasing villages in Shropshire, indeed, without disrespect it is what many people regard, usually incorrectly, as typical of the industrial northern towns, with grimy brick miners' accommodation. Located deep within the south-western area of Shropshire, Highley is not one of those places where you would regularly visit, unless calling on friends or relatives in the region. It is an area virtually free from the influence of the tourist industry.

Highley first received publicity in May 1972 when a national newspaper reported the High Court action of Mrs Selina Whittle, who was attempting to secure funds from her ex-husband's estate. George Whittle had died leaving £106,000, and while alive had given his common-law wife, Dorothy, £70,000 and three properties, and had also settled large amounts on the two children of the relationship. On learning of this from a local newspaper Mrs Selina Whittle was justly incensed, for after their divorce her husband had allowed her £2 a week, assuring her he could afford no more. So Selina took her claim to the High Court, and the publicity attendant on her action may well have triggered the tragedy that followed.

Lesley, the daughter of George and Dorothy Whittle, had received a settlement of £82,500 from her father. She was just a teenager at the time of the action, a hard-working and sensible girl. She lived with her mother, Dorothy at Beech Croft, Highley, a fine 1930s detached house. The saga of George Whittle's will was all but forgotten by the time Highley next hit the headlines in January 1975.

Dorothy Whittle was horrified when on the morning of Tuesday 14 January 1975, she became aware of Lesley's absence from Beech Croft. She searched through every room in the house but could find no trace of her daughter. Attempting to telephone her son Ronald, who also lived in Highley, she found that the telephone was not working, so she drove to his house and alerted him to Lesley's disappearance.

It was soon clear that someone had deliberately cut Dorothy's telephone wires, then a further find was made in the lounge of the house. A chocolate box containing empty sweet wrappers had been placed on top of a vase, which was not in its usual position. Within the box and wrappers were pieces of dymotape which bore a sinister message:

NO POLICE £50,000 RANSOM BE READY TO DELIVER FIRST EVENING WAIT FOR TELEPHONE CALL AT SWAN SHOPPING CENTRE TELEPHONE BOX 64711 64611 63111 6 PM TO 1 AM IF NO CALL RETURN FOLLOWING EVENING WHEN YOU ANSWER CALL GIVE YOUR NAME ONLY AND LISTEN YOU MUST FOLLOW INSTRUCTIONS WITHOUT ARGUMENT FROM

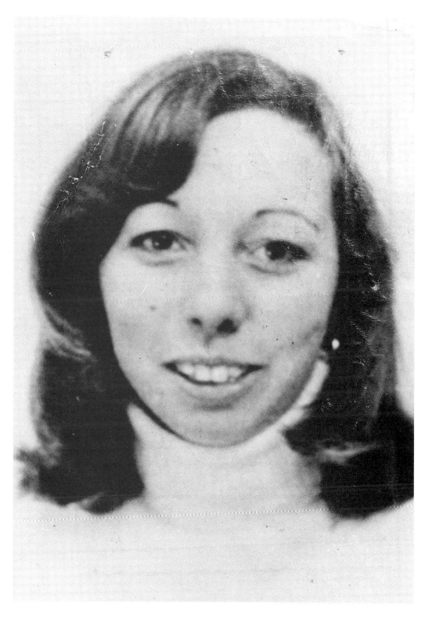

Lesley Whittle.

THE TIME YOU ANSWER THE TELEPHONE YOU ARE ON A TIME LIMIT IF POLICE OR TRICKS DEATH

There was a second tape:

£50,000 ALL IN USED NOTES £25,000 £1, £25,000 £5. THERE WILL BE NO EXCHANGE ONLY AFTER £50,000 HAS BEEN CLEARED WILL VICTIM BE RELEASED.

The police were at once notified, and Detective Chief Superintendent Booth, Head of CID, commenced investigations. A team was hurriedly assembled and an embargo placed upon any press or other public releases. However, news of the kidnap was leaked to a local journalist who quickly passed it on to the radio, who in turn announced it on the air. Further releases were prevented, and the police arranged for the relevant telephone lines to have tracers placed upon them. For one reason or another, the calls went unanswered but were traced to a telephone box in Dudley, West Midlands, some 30 miles away.

On the evening of Wednesday 15 January 1975, one day after Lesley's kidnapping, a 44 year old British Rail employee, Gerald Smith, working nightshift at Dudley found a man lurking suspiciously close to the depot. As he approached the stranger, he was shot and wounded. The gunman then calmly approached his victim, and pointed the gun at the injured man. Thankfully the weapon failed to fire and the gunman fled into the darkness.

Forensic examination of the bullets removed from the injured man's kidneys were identified as being of the same type as those used in the murders of three postmasters at different locations. It was realised that the police were dealing with one and the same individual.

On the night of 16 January, an employee of the Whittles' family coach company answered a call at Beech Croft. That it was a pay phone was obvious from the intermittent pips and the thud of the coins dropping. The voice at the other end of the line said, 'Mum, you are to go to Kidsgrove post office telephone box. The instructions are inside, behind the backboard. I'm OK but there's to be no police, no tricks, OK?'

Ronald Whittle was wired up by the police with a special mini microphone and transmitter in order that they could listen in to everything that was said, and he set off for Kidsgrove post office. After an hour or so of frantic searching of the inside of the phone box, Ronald located yet another dymotape message:

GO TO THE END OF THE ROAD AND TURN INTO BOAT HOUSE LANE GO TO THE TOP OF THE LANE AND TURN INTO

NO ENTRY GO TO THE WALL AND FLASH LIGHTS LOOK FOR TORCH RUN TO TORCH. FURTHER INSTRUCTIONS ON TORCH THEN GO HOME AND WAIT FOR TELEPHONE.

This route directed him to Bathpool Park, where in the gloom and isolation of the winter's darkness, he became disorientated and missed the rendezvous point. Once again the trail was lost.

One week later the police were notified of an abandoned vehicle parked close to Dudley bus station and terminal. Its registration read TTV 454H, and it displayed a stolen and fraudulently altered tax disc. The vehicle had in fact been stolen from West Bromwich three months previously. When the car was recovered and searched, the police found a number of items which were conclusively to prove that the person who had shot and killed three postmasters, and attempted to murder Gerald Smith in Dudley, was in fact the same person who had now kidnapped Lesley Whittle; an individual who had been named by the popular press, the Black Panther!

The car, an Austin Morris 1100/1300 type vehicle, contained amongst other items, a tape recorder and cassette, plastic sheeting, 90 feet of lorry lashing rope, a rubber and foam mattress, torch and four envelopes in which were found a number of dymotape messages. It was clear that Gerald Smith had disturbed the Panther during his deployment of the tape messages.

The cassette was played back, once again it was Lesley Whittle's voice, this time an echo was evident in the background; Lesley had been speaking whilst in an empty room. The message again provided instructions for a route to be taken where further messages would be located, and Lesley also reassured her mother that she was OK!

The Panther's trail grew cold, the search instructions on the dymotapes proved more or less fruitless, and without warning the kidnapper had seemingly gone to ground.

It was at this stage that Chief Superintendent Bob Booth played his trump card. Still confused by the dymotape trail, he decided that the best course of action was to follow the clues through again and again. It struck him that the trail had been lost in Bathpool Park, yet to order a search of the same area would alert the kidnapper that the police were involved, hence something had to be arranged to equal the cunning displayed by the Panther.

Ronald Whittle gave a television news interview in which he told how the kidnapper had drawn him to Bathpool Park, but that he had failed to make contact. This statement was prearranged by Booth in order to provide the police with a reason to become involved. House to house enquiries were carried out and suddenly vital evidence

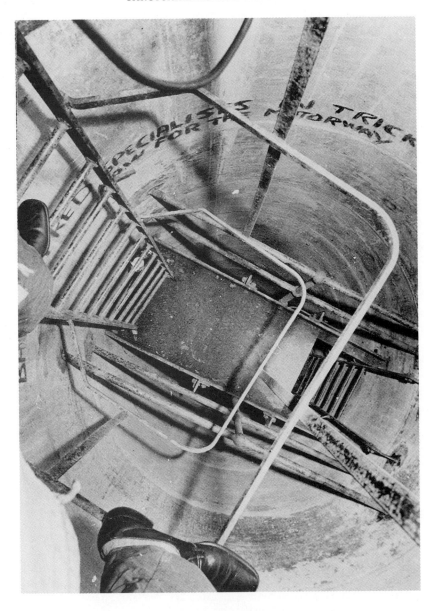

The drainage shaft.

began to emerge. It was now over 40 days since Lesley had been kidnapped, and although it was never publicly stated, everyone was seriously concerned about Lesley's welfare and the silence of her captor.

Children at play were to provide the information which was to lead to the discovery of Lesley's body. They found various dymo-tape messages in Bathpool Park, as well as a torch at the entrance to a drain shaft, more commonly known as 'The Glory Hole'. The shaft was actually one of three in the area. Booth ordered that they should be systematically searched. The first two were empty, but the third contained a grisly find. Some 50 feet below ground, on a metal grill platform, the police located a foam mattress, a sleeping bag, and a survival blanket. Flashing the torch around in this black hell an officer caught sight of a blue dressing-gown caught on the edge of the platform. Within seconds his gaze was to meet with a sight which must surely live with him for evermore – the naked body of Lesley Whittle suspended from a metal cord which was attached to her neck.

The search was over, Lesley Whittle was dead, murdered by a callous and inhumane monster, an innocent young girl destroyed by the greed of a diseased mind.

Despite further desperate enquiries, the police could find nothing which would directly relate to any suspect, yet they continued with their investigation with great enthusiasm and professionalism, refusing to allow such a killer to stay free. The press assisted in as much as they continued to report upon the continuing enquiry, thus maintaining the pressure on the Panther.

It was not until the 11th December that same year, that there were further developments. PCs White and McKenzie were on patrol in Mansfield Woodhouse at around 11 pm, when they saw a man acting in a suspicious manner near to the Four Ways public house close to old Mill Lane. He was carrying a holdall. The officers pulled up in their patrol car alongside the man, and asked him a few routine questions about where he had been and so forth; nothing unusual about such checks being made of people at this time of night, especially when they are carrying holdalls.

Initially the man was quite approachable, but suddenly produced a sawn-off shotgun and forced his way into the police car, with PC White climbing into the rear. With the shotgun barrel rammed under PC McKenzie's armpit, the Panther ordered them to drive to Blidworth. Both officers knew that they had but one chance of survival, the gunman had to be overpowered. As the car drove

A courtroom sketch of the 'Black Panther'.

through Rainsworth and along Southwell Road, White lurched forward and attempted to disarm the man. McKenzie slammed the police car brakes full on, and the mobile ground to a sudden halt outside a fish and chip shop. The gun was discharged, but only slightly injured PC White.

Two men waiting in the chip shop saw and heard the officers' cries for assistance and ran out to the car and helped overpower the man, who was then disarmed, handcuffed and secured to an iron railing fence. A search of his person and property revealed a cartridge belt with spare cartridges, two knives, one worn on a belt, the other secreted within a shoe, two razor blades, one of which had been lodged within a cigarette lighter, the other stitched into the lining of his jacket, two hoods and a bottle of ammonia. The two officers, who had by now radioed for back-up, realised that this was no ordinary criminal, both thought but never openly discussed the fact that they may have caught the Black Panther.

The man was taken to Mansfield Police Station, and later to Kidsgrove; by this stage he had been photographed and fingerprinted, his clothing had been sent for forensic examination, and information and positive proof that he was the man wanted soon became available. Yet despite this, at first he refused to co-operate. Eventually, perhaps aware that his reign was over, he told officers that his name was Donald Neilson, born 1st August 1936, and that he resided in Grangefield Avenue, Thornaby, Bradford. He denied deliberately killing Lesley Whittle.

At his trial (which was held in Oxford because it was deemed he would received a biased hearing in the Midlands), on 14th of June 1976, he was found guilty of the kidnap and murder of Lesley Whittle. His trial continued and he was also found guilty of the murder of three postmasters, and sentenced to five concurrent life sentences; in other words, he would never again be a free man, and like many other Black Panthers, is safely secured behind bars.

14

THE HILDA MURRELL CASE

THE UNSOLVED MURDER AT SHREWSBURY, MARCH 1984

Mutilation as a method of murder is a ghastly and horrendous act, especially when parts of the victim are discovered by passers-by. Perhaps the most famous mutilator of all times was Jack the Ripper, whose Victorian crimes have been theorised upon by so-called 'experts'. Many of these are mutilators of fact, destroying the truth and creating a Gothic fantasy out of the affair.

Typically, a case in Shropshire in 1984 has aroused great debate and speculation, to such a degree that the basic facts of the case have been all but forgotten in the assumptions and half baked solutions to a straightforward crime. Like the case of Jack the Ripper, the Hilda Murrell case holds no real mystery, other than the identification of the killer, there were no black magic plots, no political intrigue, no secret service assassinations, no governmental intervention to silence the affair. Hilda Murrell was murdered by a common thief, a burglar who had been disturbed, and a close look at the basic facts of the case reveals just how mutilated the story has become.

Hilda Murrell was 78 years old at the time of her sad death. She resided in Sutton Road, Shrewsbury, and lived alone. She possessed a great love of roses, and was internationally recognised as an expert rose-grower. She was also a well-known anti-nuclear campaigner and had spent some time camping outside RAF Greenham Common in Berkshire, where the deadly Cruise missiles were stored in huge bunkers as part of the European Defence system. There was nothing Miss Murrell advocated more than nature itself; she was a great believer in allowing things to happen in a natural manner without the interference of technology or outside agencies. Sadly, such idealistic opinions are now considered impractical, and although the demonstrations outside the RAF base were given high media profile, nothing was really achieved, the missiles came in, the demonstrators never got close to preventing their arrival, and simply lost their way, until they were all but forgotten, and lived as vagrants.

That is not to say that Hilda Murrell was an extremist, for many of the peace campaigners at Greenham Common were reasonable enough people, leading normal daily lives, perhaps working in the city and reaping the rewards of technological advancement yet rebelling against it during weekends. Hilda Murrell was a genuine protestor, she held firm and honest beliefs, and shared these with other women during her frequent visits to the base.

Apart from the Greenham demonstrations, which in 1984 were almost in full flow, Miss Murrell was researching for a paper which she was to present in opposition to the Sizewell B nuclear plant in Suffolk, nothing sinister or suspicious about such research, it was simply her belief that she had a right to do so.

On the morning of Wednesday 21 March 1984, Hilda Murrell left her home and went into Shrewsbury for her weekly shopping, returning home between 12 noon and 12.45 pm. There she stumbled upon an intruder who actually took Hilda Murrell from her home in her own car, a Renault, drove it to Haughmond Hill, Hunkington and told her to get out. Miss Murrell was then frogmarched and dragged 500 yards across a cornfield to Moat Copse, where she was viciously attacked and mutilated with a breadknife removed from the kitchen of her own home. The killer then left her there. Hilda Murrell died of the effects of the attack and of hypothermia.

The first intimation of the attack came when her car was found abandoned in a country lane some six miles from Shrewsbury, then her body was found in the field. From the more deviant injuries that had been inflicted on the body, the police realised that her attacker was indeed an evil sadist. A search of her home was undertaken by the authorities, and it was found to have been systematically and painstakingly searched, presumably by her killer. Money had been stolen, and some spurious claims even suggest that her report on Sizewell was missing.

The police investigation spread far and wide, posters were placed all around Shrewsbury asking for information and for people to come forward. A description of Hilda Murrell's car and registration, LNT 917W, was circulated in the hope that someone had seen the car being driven either by Miss Murrell or her attacker.

Numerous witnesses came forward, some provided sightings of the vehicle in Shrewsbury town centre at around 12.45 pm on the afternoon of the crime, being driven by a solitary male. Detective

Hilda Murrell's abandoned Renault at Haughmond Hill.

Superintendent Cole, who headed the investigation was an astute officer and fully utilised the media in the hope of flushing out the killer. Further witnesses came forward, identifying a man who was seen running away from the area where Miss Murrell's car was found abandoned, yet despite every effort, the killer has never been traced.

The lack of police success naturally led to accusations of a cover up, as acquaintances of Miss Murrell jumped on the bandwagon and saw it as another ideal opportunity of having a go at authority. Demonstrations were held at Greenham Common in remembrance of the murdered peace protestor, and it was from such sources that the mystery was invented. Talk of Miss Murrell's paper on the Sizewell nuclear plant being stolen was viewed by some as a clear indication that she had been silenced by some under-cover agency, her report adjudged to be so influential as to cause quite a stir among government circles.

Further talk told of how her nephew, Lieutenant-Commander

 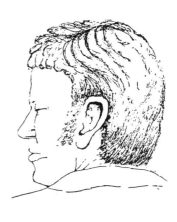

A police artist's impressions of the man seen running from the scene of the murder.

Green, was in naval intelligence, and that she possessed crucial and intimidating information upon the sinking of the *General Belgrano* cruiser during the Falklands War. None of these tales were ever proven to be accurate, but simply enhanced a little old lady's reputation. Hilda Murrell was 78 years of age, she was hardly likely to maintain a silence over any top secret and vital information she might have held. With her contacts, and bearing in mind her age, she would have acquired the assistance of others in revealing her information.

If the Government, Secret Service, Home Office, Ministry of Defence or whoever, wanted her silenced, then they selected a ridiculous manner in which to do it. Her killer remember, left her fatally wounded, but alive in that field; a paid assassin would not take such a risk. Furthermore, if the Government really did want to get rid of her, and let's face facts, there is not the slightest evidence that they did, then why not just manipulate her disappearance, instead of butchering her, leaving room for speculation?

However, if we take it that none of these agencies were involved, and that a psychopath actually killed her, then we are provided with a great deal more credibility. A burglar raiding her home is disturbed, what if she recognised him? He would have had no alternative but

A police checkpoint, set up to further their enquiries with local people.

to kill her or face a jail sentence, and in a reasonably small environment such as Shrewsbury, many reputations can be destroyed for life if one is revealed as a crook or petty thief. In such circumstances the thief would have no alternative but to destroy her. In panic he takes her out into the country where she is abused and savagely stabbed, before being left to die. These are not the actions of a trained killer but of a crazed individual. Perhaps there was more than one, certainly the killer would have had to escape from the area, and he had already dumped Hilda Murrell's car in a ditch close to her murder site; that is of course, unless they were local people who could easily make their way home!

During my research for this book, I have already received information as to local opinion, some of which is extremely interesting. Obviously, if anyone else can provide information please feel free to do so, as I hope in the very near future to cover the case in its entirety, but this is clearly dependent upon any information

114

which may be forthcoming.

From what I have so far researched, it would seem that apart from the killer, someone somewhere knows a lot more than they are letting on. So many people approached me upon this one case that it was impossible not to include it within the pages of this casebook. A whole community still feels a great deal of despair and anguish over the Murrell murder, a lack of understanding as to why the killer has never been brought to justice. Yet the police have done everything within their powers to achieve success, investigations and enquiries still continue to this day.

Hilda Murrell's killer could be and probably is, alive and well. If you are that person and you are reading this, then remember, there is no such thing as the perfect crime, to date you have been fortunate, but never underestimate the powers of law and order; as time progresses, the net is closing. Yours must be a difficult conscience, perhaps ten years later you are now ready to unburden yourself. Until you do so, the search will never cease!

15

THE HEATH HOUSE MURDER MYSTERY

THE UNSOLVED MURDER OF SIMON DALE
AT HOPTON HEATH, SEPTEMBER 1987

In 1968 a relatively straightforward murder occurred in the
beautiful surroundings of the Shropshire countryside, a crime
which was so senseless, so pointless, yet one man's desperate plight
forced him to the inaccurate conclusion that destruction of another
life was the best way of resolving his personal problem.

Arthur Prime was not what you would call a callous man; in actual
fact his loyalties and total devotion were directed towards his wife,
who in 1968 was not in the best of health. Mrs Prime's physical
condition deteriorated despite the desperate efforts of her general
practitioner Dr Alan Beach.

Sadly she died, leaving her husband to deal with his personal grief.
Arthur Prime was devastated by the loss of his most prized
possession, he found it difficult to accept that she had now gone and
he was a widower. Prime spent many restless hours pondering over
his wife's death, and his disturbed mind began to brood on distorted
images. He dwelt on his own personal guilt. What if he had done
things differently? Could it, would it have saved his wife? A stress-
free, logical mind would of course have dismissed such thoughts, but
Arthur was a man in deep mourning; grief, anger and crazed thoughts
filled his distraught mind, until eventually he found someone to
shoulder the responsibility for his wife's death!

Dr Alan Beach was sitting in his car at the entrance gate to Heath
House when he was shot dead by Arthur Prime in a bizarre act of
revenge, with Prime laying the blame for his wife's death upon her
doctor! Prime was of course totally devoid of reasoned thought
when he committed this atrocious act; he was tried and found guilty

Simon Dale outside the main doorway of Heath House.

of murder and sentenced to life imprisonment which was spent in a psychiatric unit.

Most rural environments never have to suffer the distress of a murder and the subsequent unwanted media attention it creates. Thankfully the Beach murder was played down and one would imagine that the peaceful tranquillity of the Hopton Heath area would have returned, and so it did, but it was to be a brief respite, for less than 20 years later murder revisited Heath House, only this time the mystery remains, ensuring that it holds its own entry in the records of the country's unsolved crime annals.

Simon Dale was a 68 year old partially sighted, retired architect who lived alone in Heath House, an old Jacobean mansion. He was enthusiastically interested in a variety of subjects including archaeology and general history, subjects that became his main lifeline with the outside world as he avidly penned several magazine and journal articles. Suffering from inadequate eyesight Dale employed a team of helpers for different tasks. Giselle Wall generally typed his manuscripts and helped out with general chores. Dale had a number of such persons whom he would call upon when necessary.

Giselle called at Heath House on Sunday 13th September 1987; it was close to 4.30 pm when she arrived to discuss with Dale the latest manuscript she was preparing. As she entered the premises she noticed that the wooden shutters were closed, most unusual for Dale, especially on such a pleasant autumn afternoon. Inside she was greeted by the most horrific scene she was ever likely to encounter. Laid upon the floor of the kitchen on his back was the corpse of Simon Dale, blood splattered surrounding walls and a large crimson pool surrounded his head, the cooker was switched on and food which was being prepared by Dale was burnt to a cinder. The heat in the kitchen was overwhelming and the sickening stench of death filled the air. Giselle fled for help and within minutes the emergency services had arrived at the scene.

The first task was to certify Dale's death. With that achieved, it was then the role of the investigating officers to commence their exhaustive enquiries. Detective Superintendent David Cole formed his team for the investigation and was at once confronted with several matters which did not fit into the anticipated pattern usually associated with such an attack. The obvious motive was burglary, a would-be intruder having been disturbed by Dale who was then bludgeoned to death in blind panic. Yet the corpse still displayed the gold cufflinks placed on the shirt earlier that fateful day, and in the back pocket of the trousers was a wallet containing money. Additionally, a slightly less suspicious fact, there was no sign of forced entry albeit there was no security barrier for any would-be intruder to overcome. Doors were often left unlocked by Dale. Those facts considered, a motive was not immediately apparent.

Giselle Wall and other local residents were interviewed by the police in an attempt to gain some local knowledge of and background on Dale; his movements, his visitors, his business interests, his family.

Dale had been married, his ex-wife was now known as Baroness Susan de Stempel; she resided in Docklow, almost 30 miles from Heath House. It was further ascertained that there was little if any love lost between Dale and the Baroness, who had gained her title from a later marriage which also failed, though she afterwards managed to retain her title.

Police called in at the Baroness's home initially to inform her of the death of her ex-husband, an unpleasant task bearing in mind the circumstances. However, the trained eye and knowledge of an experienced police officer detected a little more to the Baroness than he expected. For a start there was no grief, and very little if any other emotion, a factor which immediately alerted the vigilant officer's attention and suspicions.

Having spoken to the Baroness and her three grown up children, Marcus, Sophia and Simon junior, all from her relationship with Simon Dale, and further identified a link with a Lady Margaret Illingworth via personal mail in the Baroness's cottage, the officer left. Before doing so he noticed a brass poker which lay in a car outside the cottage, and took possession of this as it was an unusual object to keep in one's private car. Another interesting factor noted by those officers visiting the Baroness's home that night was the number of antiques present on the premises; for such a modest property it was packed with obviously expensive furniture and other valuables.

The forensic department had been hard at work at Heath House and it was quickly identified that Dale had not been murdered the day on which he had been found. The body had lain in the intense heat of the kitchen with the oven turned on full and little if any outside ventilation; this heat had ensured that decomposition took place quite quickly. Experiments were carried out in an attempt to see how long such decomposition would have taken in such an atmosphere by using dead animals. Tests were made of the charred food in the oven and scientists eventually claimed that Simon Dale must have died between 8.30 pm and 9.00 pm on the night of Friday 11 September 1987.

Armed with this new information the police could now attempt to track down everyone who was known to have visited Heath House on that particular day. The Baroness and two of her children had been there working on the exterior decoration of the house, which was not unusual as the family had done so for several months prior to the murder, maintaining the outer decor as Dale was himself incapable of doing so.

The Baroness had not objected to this as she was in dispute with Dale over her right to ownership of the property, which presumably after Dale's death would be left to their children. It was therefore in everyone's best interest that the property was correctly maintained. However such was the animosity between the pair that the Baroness and Dale spent little if any time alone. There was even some suggestion that the Baroness feared that Dale might physically attack her.

Other visitors to the premises included close friends of Dale who were also interested in archaeology. These people left the premises at around 8.15 pm that night, as they had two young children with them.

At this time, the Baroness and her son Marcus remained in the grounds. Sophia, her daughter, had left some time earlier going directly home. Marcus tended to some beehives before again joining his mother, then they both left for the journey home, claiming that they arrived there shortly after 9 pm.

Before the murder enquiry could make any significant headway a further complication transpired involving the arrest of the Baroness de Stempel and her children Marcus and Sophia, as well as her previous husband, Baron Michael de Stempel. In December 1987 they were arrested on suspicion of fraud. It was later revealed that Lady Illingworth had been an extremely wealthy lady, who had come to stay with Baroness de Stempel at Docklow a few years previously. It appeared that the de Stempels had syphoned off Lady Illingworth's wealth and all of her antiques before putting her in a Hereford old people's home where she died in 1986. Her will, made out in 1986, left the majority of her estate to the Baroness!

Despite this unfortunate, or perhaps some may say, fortunate intervention the murder investigation had to continue. The Baroness had already told police officers that when at Heath House she would carry with her a crow-bar or jemmy, not solely as protection against Dale but also as a useful aid to knocking down obstructive nettles

Detective Superintendent David Cole is surprised by a question from a member of the press corps in the grounds of Heath House.

and thorn bushes. This seemed a remarkably odd tool for such a task. It was subjected to various forensic tests but no blood or hair could be found attached to its metal surfaces.

Public announcements were made by the police requesting members of the public to come forward with any information no matter how irrelevant it might seem, as every little helped. This only confused matters further as there was a report of a suspicious red car parked on the roadside near Heath House with its occupants looking in the direction of the mansion! A further report claimed that a man, a stranger to the district, was seen close by, but despite these sightings there was very little in the way of clear-cut evidence.

The investigation continued, with the media attention dwindling to disinterest until the January of 1988 when it was announced that Baroness de Stempel, Marcus and Sophia had been arrested on suspicion of murder. This was in conjunction with the fraud charge which all three faced together with Baron Michael de Stempel! As subsequent enquiries continued there was insufficient evidence to charge Marcus and Sophia with the murder, but it stood against the Baroness.

There were a number of suspicious factors to be taken into consideration in relation to the Baroness being the killer, the first of which was the means of access to the premises. It was definitely a fact that the Baroness was seen in the grounds of the house after the last visitors had. left. In this respect, she claimed that she felt it her duty to remain to ensure that all was well with the property and with her ex-husband Simon.

Five sherry glasses had been left on the kitchen table, one of which was damaged and unable to hold liquid. Four of the glasses were known to have been used by Simon Dale and his earlier visitors while discussing archaeology; but who had drunk out of the fifth glass? A single individual who must have been known to Simon Dale, otherwise why would he offer them a drink in his kitchen? By the Baroness's own admission, there was no one else at the premises when she left, which according to the scientific tests was the approximate time of Dale's death. Furthermore, she was alone for a short while when her son Marcus tended to the beehives.

The Baroness admitted visiting the premises the day after the murder, yet she broke her routine of parking her car, a Peugeot Estate, to the rear of the premises. Instead, she parked it at the front and ensured that her younger son Simon was with her as she tended to the garden. She claimed that although she noticed that the shutters were closed over the windows she did not think it suspicious, and anyway, if she had entered the house she would have left herself exposed to a possible assault from her ex-husband.

Then there was the absolute hate between Dale and herself. Since their break-up she had attempted to get Dale to sell the property in order that the proceeds could be split between them. Dale had been dilatory in this respect, a factor which further angered her. There were also allegations that she had openly wished him dead; though this could hardly be seen as direct evidence of her actually murdering him.

At the subsequent murder trial, Baroness Susan de Stempel was found not guilty of the murder of her ex-husband Simon Dale. The evidence was insufficient to convict her; however she still faced prosecution for the fraud charge.

The trial for fraud took place in Birmingham in February 1990 lasting ten weeks. The Baroness pleaded guilty to seven charges of fraud and was sentenced to seven years' custodial sentence. Marcus de Stempel was sentenced to 18 months for his part in the fraud and Sophia two years and six months imprisonment. Baron Michael de Stempel received a four year jail sentence.

At the time of writing the murder of Simon Dale remains unsolved, though the case has not been closed and investigations continue. For some, life can be extremely cruel, with memories of the past flooding back to mind, haunting us, refusing, unlike human beings to die. For those left behind, the mental torture of a suspicious death can prove destructive.

Index

Acton Burnell   26
Alcoholism and
   murder   88-94
Aldermaston   35
Angel hotel, Ludlow   20-21
Asphyxiation   100-109
Atcham   81-87
Atcherley, Major Llewellyn   31
Axe murders   58-63

Bathpool Park   105, 106, 107
Bathurst, Dr   52, 53
Beach, Dr Alan   116
Becke, Major Jack   32-33
Bicton   93
Biggs, Diana   23-24
Bishop's Castle   97
'Black Panther, The'   100-109
Bolderston, PC   52, 54
Booth, Det Chief Supt   104,
   105, 107
Borden, Lizzie   58
Bowen, Eliza   42-47
Bridgnorth   19, 26, 29, 38
Bronygarth   21-23
Bufton, William   95-99
Burford   29
Burgwin, Benjamin   25
Burroughs, Sir
   Nehemiah   13-14.

Carver, Caroline and
   Charles   65-70
Catnach, Jeremy   12
Cefn Mawr (North Wales)   22

Chief Constables, Shropshire
Force
   Atcheley, Major Llewellyn
   31
   Becke, Major John   32-33
   Crampton, Capt Philip
      Henry   27
   Cureton, Lt Col Edward
      Burgoyne   27-28
   Derriman, Capt Gerald
      31-32
   Edgell, Col Richard   28, 30
   Fenwick, Robert   33
   Golden, Capt Harold   33
   Mayne, Capt Dawson   19,
      26, 27
   Ormond, Douglas   33
   Williams-Freeman, Capt
      George   30, 31
Churchbank   95-99
Church Stretton   29, 58-63
Clewes, Dorothy   72-76
Clun   95, 96
Cole, Det Supt David   112,
   118, 121
Colley, Charles   26
Constables, origin of   15-16,
   37-38
Cooke, Susannah   50-53
Copthorne   82, 88-94
Cound   43-45
Crampton, Capt Philip   27
Crime investigation
   procedures   39-41
Cross Houses   43, 45

Cureton, Lt Col
  Edward 27-28

Dale, Marcus 119, 120, 122,
  123
Dale, Simon 117-123
Dale, Sophia 119, 120, 122
Davies, Mr and Mrs
  John 55-57
Davies, Mary 17-18
Davies, William 27
de Stempel, Baron
  Michael 120, 122, 123
de Stempel, Baroness
  Susan 119-123
Derriman, Capt Gerald 31-32
Docklow 119, 120
Dorrington 17
Doughty family 60-53
Drowning 64-70
Dudley 24, 104, 105

Edgell, Col Richard John 28,
  30
Edgmond 65-70
Evans, Ann 26-27
Evans, Emma 21-23

Fenwick, Robert 33
Freeman, Richard 25

General Belgrano cruiser 113
Golden, Capt Harold 33
Goodall, PC 38-39
Green, Lt
  Commander 112-113
Greenham Common 110-111,
  112
Gwynne, John 81

Hall, Tony 33
Hanging, death by 100-109

Harlescott 90
Harwood, Jocelin 12-14
Haughmond Hill 111
Heath House murder,
  The 116-123
Highley 101-109
Hill, Ernest Robert 72-76
Holmes, Harold 60-61, 62
Home Office Large Major
  Enquiry System
  (HOLMES) 40
Hooper, Desmond
  Donald 82-87
Hopton Heath 116-123
'Hue and cry' 16-17
Hunkington 111
Hutchins, Harvey 14-15

Illingworth, Lady
  Margaret 119, 120
Infanticide 49-54

Jack the Ripper 29, 36, 42,
  110
Jones, John 23-24

Kidsgrove 104
King's Head, Cefn Mawr 22

Lewis, Superintendent 24, 25,
  57
Lion, The (Westbury) 43-47
  passim
Llanfair 44
Llwney Mapsis 18
Lowndes, Clara
  Elizabeth 50-54
Ludlow 19, 20, 21
Ludlow, John 20

McKenzie, PC 107-109
Mackereth, William 20-21

Mansfield   109
Mansfield Woodhouse   107
Market Drayton   71-76 *passim*
Martin, Olive   93
Mayne, Capt Dawson   19, 26, 27
Micklewright, PC John   26
Minsterley   77-80
Mister, Joseph   20-21
Moreton Say   73
Moreton Wood   72
Much Wenlock   26
Murrell, Hilda   110-115
Myott, Dr Edgar
   Conningsby   75

Neilson, Donald ('Black
   Panther')   100-109
Newport   65-69 *passim*

Ormond, Douglas   33
Oswestry   18, 19, 21, 29, 49, 55-57
Overfield, Mr & Mrs
   Richard   38-39
Owen, George   97-99

Pen-y-Wern   95
Perkins, Edward and
   Thomas   77-80
Petton   49-54
Phipps, Thomas   18-19
Pierrepoint, Henry   47
Pigeon fancying   82-83
Police – early days   15-21, 37
      20th century   21-34
Pontesbury   29, 36-37
Pontesford   37
Pontypool, Wales   24
Porton Down   35
Preece, Elisabeth   36-37
Prime, Arthur   116, 118

Rhos Cottage murder   95-99
Riley, George   89-94
Roberts, Inspector
   Charles   61, 62
Rolfe, Det Sergeant   29
Rudge, PC   52, 54
Ruxton, Dr Buck   71-72

Scene of Crime Officers
   (SOCO)   35, 40
Severn, river   81, 82
Shot-gun murders   71-76, 95-99
Shrewsbury   12-25 *passim*, 29, 43-49 *passim*, 77, 79, 81, 86, 88, 90, 94, 97, 110-115
Shropshire Union Canal   66-69
   passim, 84
Sizewell B nuclear plant   111, 112
Slawson, William   21-23
Smith, Elizabeth Selina   33-87
Smith, Gerald   104, 105
Smith, PC Jeremiah   25
Smith, Mrs (of
   Copthorne)   92-94
Speake, PC Henry   33
Stafford   94
Stokesay   23-24
Strangulation   81-87

Tern Hill   72-73
Throat-cutting   42-47
Toothache murder   77-80
Turner, Sarah   17-18

Upton Magna   25

Venables, Jennifer   95-99

Wall, Giselle   118, 119
Wappenstall   68

Wellington   28, 29, 43
Wells, Charlie   95, 96-97
Wem   25
Wenlock   19
Westbury   42-47
West Mercia Constabulary,
   formation of   34
Whitchurch   29
White, PC   107-109
Whittle, Dorothy   102

Whittle, George   102-109
Whittle, Lesley   102-109
Whittle, Ronald   102-105
Whittle, Selina   102
Wigley, Richard   43-48
Williams-Freeman, Capt
   George   30, 31
Williams, John   21-23
Wrexham   22, 49